INFLUENTIAL MACHINES

INFLUENTIAL MACHINES

THE RHETORIC OF COMPUTATIONAL PERFORMANCE

MILES C. COLEMAN

© 2023 University of South Carolina

Published by the University of South Carolina Press
Columbia, South Carolina 29208

uscpress.com

Manufactured in the United States of America

32 31 30 29 28 27 26 25 24 23
10 9 8 7 6 5 4 3 2 1

Library of Congress Cataloging-in-Publication Data
can be found at http://catalog.loc.gov/.

ISBN: 978-1-64336-458-2 (hardcover)
ISBN: 978-1-64336-459-9 (paperback)
ISBN: 978-1-64336-460-5 (ebook)

This book will be made open access within three years of publication thanks to
Path to Open, a program developed in partnership between JSTOR, the American
Council of Learned Societies (ACLS), University of Michigan Press, and The University
of North Carolina Press to bring about equitable access and impact for the entire
scholarly community, including authors, researchers, libraries, and university
presses around the world. Learn more at https://about.jstor.org/path-to-open/

For Ash and Bash

CONTENTS

List of Tables and Figures viii
Acknowledgments ix

Introduction: Locating the Energies of
Computational Performance 1

CHAPTER 1
Manufactured Processing, Ritual, and Expert Systems 24

CHAPTER 2
Processual Magnitude, the Sublime, and Computational Poiesis 45

CHAPTER 3
Processual Signaling, Compulsion, and Neural Networks 62

CHAPTER 4
Designing Computational Performances to Actively
Contribute Positive Energies 88

CHAPTER 5
Leveraging the Rhetorical Energies of Machines 110

Notes 125
Works Cited 139
Index 157

TABLES AND FIGURES

Tables

TABLE 0.1 Traditional and Computational Performances 8

TABLE 0.2. Distinctions Between Procedurality and Rhetorical Energies in an Analysis of a Carbon Footprint Calculator 21

TABLE 1.1. Hepatitis B Excerpt from VaxCalc-Labs "Vaccine-Ingredients-Data" 36

TABLE 1.2. List of Selections from "Step Two" of Vaccine Calculator 37

Figures

FIGURE 1.1. CDC Catch-Up Immunization Landing Page 31

FIGURE 1.2. CDC Catch-Up Vaccination Scheduler Output 31

FIGURE 1.3. CDC Child and Adolescent Vaccine Assessment User Input Page 34

FIGURE 3.1. The Performance of @DeepDrumpf 82

FIGURE 3.2. @DeepDrumpf's Automated Exergasia 83

FIGURE 3.3. The Verisimilitude of the Machinic Parody of @DeepDrumpf 85

ACKNOWLEDGMENTS

Burning sage and rubbing crystals, coding interactive art installations, giving words of encouragement, leaving edit lines in a document, grooving to math rock, posting custom memes to the group chat—over the course of writing this book, I have had the pleasure not only of developing ideas, but also of personal growth, stirred by the warm, wise energies of colleagues, friends, and family. People who, in their own valuably unique ways, have taught me, and continue to teach me, what it means to imbue positive energies.

This project got its start when I was an instructor in the program on Digital Technology and Cultures at Seattle University. While there, my fellow faculty members, Shawn Ryder and Becky Peltz, accomplished web developers and scholars, generously shared with me their knowledge of coding and their seemingly effortless ability to connect humanities issues to computing. Shawn and Becky taught me how to write and read code in a way that is mindful of the influence one's application might have, something that would become an important component of my own approach to thinking rhetorically about computation. During this time, I also met my now longtime friend, Mark Anthoney, a technically inclined, gifted thinker, who worked in the Center for Digital Learning and Innovation, the instructional design unit at Seattle University. Mark's enthusiasm for the "woowoo" of technology would inspire some of the themes of this book. It was during a code art exhibition, organized by Jackie Buttice at Seattle University, featuring installations made by Jackie, Shawn, Becky, Mark, and myself, that I started to first congeal the idea for this book. Watching their installations *move* was bewildering, astonishing, and gripping—they all, in their own distinct craftiness, leveraged the movements of machines, showing what computational performances can do. Without these friendships and experiences, this book likely never would have materialized.

What started out as an inkling eventually developed into a couple of journal articles and then snowballed into a book project, informed by insightful

x   Acknowledgments

conversations with, and encouragement from, wonderful people. The conversations I had with my Seattle University colleagues Dung Tran, Trish Henley, and Rick Fehrenbacher were some of the most "far out," engaging conversations of my life. Robot Jesus! Medieval digital culture! Their challenges, ideas, and just plain exciting thinking helped me to start thinking about "machinic rhetorics" in the earlier, nascent stages of my working through the themes of the book. My Rowan University colleagues and friends, John Feaster, Amy Reed, Joy Cypher, Dan Strasser, and Dan Schowalter have graciously entertained too many "what about this" discussions in addition to generously providing written comments and feedback on earlier drafts of chapters and ideas from the book. My friends Will Mari, Jeremy Gordon, John Crowley, Melba Vélez Ortiz, Blake Ragland, Nanda Saczawa, and Joe Hanson all patiently, and warmly, prodded with insightful questions and suggestions regarding the conceptualization of the energies of computational performance (the central focus of the book). I hope that someday I can live up to what my friends and colleagues consistently model in their daily lives—compassion, capability, and positivity.

I would also like to acknowledge my doctoral and masters advisors and teachers, Leah Ceccarelli, Matt McGarrity, Mark Williams, Michelle Foss-Snowden, and Raymond Koegel, for sharing their zeal and their smarts with me. You changed my life. In addition, thanks are owed to Aurora Bell for her excellent editorship and guidance as well as the anonymous reviewers for their thoughtful commentary, suggestions, and challenges.

Most important, I would like to thank my family for their support throughout the writing of the book. Mom, you have consistently been a positive influence in my life, ever since I was a kid; now I call you to talk about whatever, including robot rhetorics! Ash and Bash—my pillars—I would not have been able to write this book without your encouragement and support. Ashley, I love everything that you do. I love your jokes, your voice, your face, your thoughts, and the way you sleep (yes, I watch you when you sleep). I love that you are you, always. You are the star in my galaxy, soaking everything around you in a life-giving light. Sebastian, at the time of this writing you are exactly 10 months old, and you are already the most amazing person. I feel like you teach me something new every day about finding wonder and joy in even the smallest, most easily overlooked nooks and crannies of a good life. I am so proud to be your father.

Parts of the introduction and chapter 3 are derived from my article, "Machinic Rhetorics and the Influential Movements of Robots," published in *The Review of Communication* (2018), copyright © National Communication

Association, available online, https://doi.org/10.1080/15358593.2018.1517417. The introduction and chapter 5 include parts of another of my articles, "Leveraging the Rhetorical Energies of Machines: COVID-19, Misinformation, and Persuasive Labor," published in *Human-Machine Communication* (2021), available online, https://doi.org/10.30658/hmc.3.2.

Introduction

Locating the Energies of
Computational Performance

Dated to the high Middle Ages, the *Lokapannati*, a text written in Pali (a sacred Buddhist language), tells a tale of steampunk robots, reincarnation, and technological power.[1] In the fantastical story, King Ajataśatru solicits the help of an engineer, knowledgeable about the Roman tradition of making self-moving machines. With the engineer's assistance, he creates a set of robot guards to protect a collection of Buddhist relics stored in a *stupa* (an underground hollow covered with a clay dome). According to popular interpretation, King Ajataśatru did this because he needed agents that could move as if they were alive, but who would also remain "unattached" to the relics, so they would be available when the rightful inheritor—King Aśoka—came to collect. Though they could not speak, Ajataśatru's robots were treated as "spirit movement machines" infused with their own anima (wind of life), a feat allegedly well-guarded by the Romans as a trade secret.[2] The story of King Ajataśatru's robots is informative in that, despite lacking speech, the robots communicated. Their *movements* embodied nodal, ambient echoes of the cultural moment in which they were being witnessed. While the ancient Romans might have gazed at the robots as feats of "spring-and-compression-propelled machinery," those same moving machines, for an ancient Indian Buddhist, might have intuited a discerning removal of the problem of "becoming attached."[3] King Ajataśatru's robots, while not alive, nonetheless moved in lively ways—they were performing. As such, they enlivened discourse by imbuing it with more-than-human rhetorical energies, which interacted with culturally shaped bodies, manifesting force not just as ideas, but as feelings.

Flash forward to today. We find similarly influential communication in computing machines. But they are not the stuff of legend. Web applications

2 Influential Machines

offer us conclusions about science. Twitter bots generate art. Machine-learning systems make fun of politicians. We live in an era where a substantial share of our public communication is machinic.[4] Like the robots of King Ajataśatru's caves, our modern computing machines cannot speak for themselves per se, but they do exert energies, which can impact persons viscerally, preconsciously. Current scholarship, in the spirit of rhetoric of science, technology, and medicine, and that field's drive to critically engage the monolith of "objective" communication, is turning attention to investigate how software can constrain, or open up, possibilities of rhetorical invention and how we might participate with automated systems to make meaning. And as a consequence, the current literature productively complicates the idea that automated technologies are neutral, passive tools, proposing instead that machines are better understood as ethically loaded, active agents (or actants) helping to comprise the assemblages of rhetorical processes. Not yet pursued at length in the current literature are the rhetorical energies that attend the performances of computing machines as they give advice, entertain, and proffer insight, speaking to human concerns in more-than-human ways. This book is an effort to better capture the opportunities and threats of influence inherent to dynamic computational media—media that can perform for users by carrying out operations "on their own." Over the course of the book, I will build out a conceptual framework useful for naming, analyzing, and evaluating the physical and emotional energies imbued within computational performances.

While applying the idea of rhetorical energy to the performances of web applications, bots, and voice-based interfaces is the unique contribution of this book, the idea of rhetorical energy itself is not new. George Kennedy first proposed that we think of rhetoric as energy in his 1992 essay, "A Hoot in the Dark," in which he explores what he calls a "general rhetoric," or a rhetoric that is not moored in the language, rationality, and intention that we so often equate with human activity, but rather more generally in the energies that impact bodies, including nonhuman ones.[5] In his words: "Rhetoric in the most general sense may perhaps be identified with the energy inherent in communication: the emotional energy that impels the speaker to speak, the physical energy expended in the utterance, the energy level coded in the message, and the energy experienced by the recipient in decoding the message."[6] Defined as such, we can recognize that humans are not the only ones that influence others. Flowers communicate desirability with sweet smells, deer communicate position within their social order with displays of strength, and crows sound calls

3 Introduction

to bring the flock together in congregation. An important point that Kennedy drives home in his essay is that rhetoric is not exclusive to humans, and, perhaps more profoundly, rhetoric is not fixed solely in the verbal or the rational. Rather, at its base, rhetoric is moored in emotional and physical energies as they are expended and experienced, shaped by biology and culture (including that of nonhuman animals).

Though Kennedy's original discussion of rhetorical energy is interested in locating the energies shared between specific living species (e.g., the suasions of crows), the idea of rhetorical energy is useful for thinking through the communication of computing machines. In the same way that Kennedy pointed our attention beyond human communication to learn more about the rhetoric of nonhuman living things, we can take it a step further by interrogating the rhetorical energy of things that are lively but not alive, such as computational performances. In fact, Kennedy probably did not have computing machines in mind, but he indirectly makes a connection between rhetorical energy and electrical current in his joking proposal of *rheme*, a unit "analogous to an erg or volt," with which the "experimentalists" could measure rhetorical energy.[7] Kennedy's passing statement demonstrates a broad-thinking quip, acknowledging the sometimes hard divides between social scientific and interpretive approaches to scholarship, but it also expresses the possibility of rhetoric in configurations not just in animal–animal scenarios, but also in animal–nonanimal scenarios. The key here is in the expenditure and experience of energy. Computing machines, as they run processes, flip switches, create states on a drive, and retrieve memory are expending energy—they are performing as computing machines. And these performances affect us.

As will be discussed in more detail later in this chapter, orienting to the rhetorical energies of computational performances is a means of thickening accounts of procedurality, something that many would identify as the defining characteristic of computational media. In *procedural rhetorics* the analyst accounts for procedures—the mechanics and decision trees of a given piece of software—in an effort to "read" the argument that it encourages onto users not through words or visuals per se, but through the processes of a given software. Procedural approaches, while often yielding profound and useful insights, also tend to emphasize logic at the expense of understanding other aspects of rhetorical influence in computing, such as feelings. This book offers a necessary thickening of procedurality by turning attention to the visceral "more" that attends the movements of computational performances, which are surely

4 Influential Machines

punctuated by procedures, but which also influence at a gestural level, shaped by a deep complex of affective/cultural layerings, accessible through the lens of rhetoric as energy.

Exploring the rhetorical energies of computational performance is an activity that joins arms with other scholars who are working to expand assumptions about what rhetoric is and how it occurs by looking beyond (human) intention, rationality, and verbally based discourses.[8] Such is a move away from rhetoric as epistemic and toward rhetoric as ontological, a distinction that Scot Barnett and Casey Boyle elaborate in their edited volume, *Rhetoric, Through Everyday Things:* "Whereas epistemology emphasizes knowledge *about* things, and thus about their meaning and cultural significance for us, ontology stresses relational *being*."[9] Integral to Barnett and Boyle's framing of rhetoric as ontological is an emphasis on embodied experience as it happens between humans and nonhumans, which pushes not only where one might look for influence, but also how influence happens in the first place. For example, in approaching rhetoric as ontological one might push on Aristotelian commitments to locating rhetoric as formal arguments or defining rhetoric as an exclusively human enterprise—to ask, like John Muckelbaurer does, whether "plants turning toward the sun and audiences accepting an argument might well involve the same kind of action/motion," complicating distinctions between symbolic and natural processes.[10] Approaching rhetoric as energy, moreover, is to follow Muckelbaurer in his provocative proposition to consider rhetoric as "heliotropic," a move that blurs the Burkean distinctions between (symbolic) action as "behavior possible to a typically symbol-using animal" and (natural) motion as "the extrasymbolic or nonsymbolic operations of nature."[11] What conceptualizing rhetoric as energy does in this sense is push toward rhetoric as ontological by locating influence beyond mere symbolism and its attending prioritization of rationality, and instead locate it between action and motion, within the expenditure and experience of energy "at work," illuminating influence in realms where we might otherwise be reluctant to concede it. Computational performances exist in our homes, the workplace, and in the public, touching nearly every aspect of our lives. This book will show that they influence in ways that are subtly powerful, for their lively (but not alive) movements complicate common assumptions regarding symbols and sensation, artificiality and naturality, and subjects and objects.

By the end of the book, I hope that the reader will come to understand that people can "catch feels" from the energies of computing machines.[12] The case studies in particular will demonstrate that computational performances

5 Introduction

are attended by influential energies that can be leveraged to catalyze sublime artistic experiences, generate false confidence in pseudoscience, and encourage compulsive reactions in politics. In an era where we increasingly communicate with our machines, rather than through them, it is paramount that we understand the energies that attend their performances. In recognizing the rhetorical energies of computing machines, we can begin to appreciate their visceral but deep suasions as well as to account for the ethical implications of their lively performances. Because people can (consciously or unconsciously) deploy the energies of machines to influence, diving deep into computing's affective / cultural layerings is not simply fun or interesting—it is integral to updating our critical sensibilities of the world.

The Rhetorical Energies of Computing Machines

Voice-based assistants, chatbots, art-making machine-learning systems—our contemporary machines can put words together, respond to their human counterparts, and generate imagery. Even in such examples, where machines are obviously communicating, some may harbor a reservation in calling it real communication and think of it as quasi-communication.[13] Such is a common view within the burgeoning field of human–machine communication, an interdisciplinary area of research, which focuses on the implications of machine communicators (such as chatbots or voice-based assistants). For example, as Leopoldina Fortunati and Autumn P. Edwards, editors of *Human-Machine Communication,* explain in their introduction to the inaugural issue of the journal:

> Humans are aware that media agents and social robots are *quasi*-interlocutor, *quasi*-communicator, *quasi*-social, but they play the game and pretend to really communicate and to have social relationships with them. . . . The strength of this illusion depends on the simulating ability of the media agents. Although it is an illusion, and is even consciously recognized as such by the people involved, it can generate all the same feelings of communicative and social satisfaction as interactions with other *humans.*[14]

The specific contributions that a rhetorical energies approach offers to human–machine communication will be discussed in more detail in the conclusion of the book. For now, we note that voice-based assistants, or chatbots, or even machine-learning systems (which can be much more autonomous in their behavior) are often conceptualized as miming symbolic interaction, for they are

6 Influential Machines

not alive like persons are. This is hard to deny—talking to a computer is talking to a computer and not a person. The computer does not have feelings or stakes in the world—it just drives forward, carrying out its scripts, and reacting to the input of a human (or another machine). And so, computing machines might be understood as agents mindlessly miming symbolic interaction, rather than engaging in real communication.

However, the "quasi" in quasi-communication is loaded with the assumption that real communication is derived from the human. What we overlook in our search for the human is an entire world of energy that matters, buzzing in the background, affecting us, covered over by a narcissistic hubris, wherein homo sapiens (the "wise" ones) look only for the voice, performance, and words of other humans as if everything else is The Nothing. While they might not have stakes in the world, or even experience feelings themselves, machines move us. And, surely, if we are looking for symbolic interactions between persons, we are forced to imagine such communication as quasi.

Yet if we adjust our definition of rhetoric, say, by following Kennedy in his proposal to think of rhetoric not as based in language or argument, or even as solely the enterprise of humans, but rather as "the *energy* inherent in communication" the persuasiveness of machines *as machines* begins to emerge.[15] Rhetorical energy can include language, but it also includes such things as "physical actions, facial expressions, gestures, and signs generally."[16] What makes Kennedy's contribution particularly distinctive is his interrogation of the rhetorics of nonhuman animals, which are not located in language per se, but rather in performances. Bucks, demonstrating their rank in the deer social order through public displays of strength—that is rhetorical energy. Flowers making appeals to honeybees with sweet smells—that is rhetorical energy too. The crux of rhetoric as energy is that it locates influence not in language but more broadly in the energies that are "at work" in the interaction between entities. Relocating influence in this way, as Chris Ingraham elaborates, jaunts the analyst into "the biologically hardwired realm of pre-intentional survival mechanisms, those that are communicated through a perceivable code, yes, but not necessarily in symbolic messages governed by a semiotic regime of meaning."[17] Likewise, Catherine Chaput and Crystal Broch Colombini center rhetorical energy as concerned with "the physiological urge to defend, sustain, and thrive . . . our most taken-for-granted modes of engagement."[18] Put differently, while our visceral responses to the world—and the other entities that imbue it with energy—might be "read," they are also nonconscious, born of entanglements of biology and culture. Although Kennedy is largely concerned with the

7 Introduction

prospect of locating rhetoric in the realms of nonhuman animals—entities that are alive—it does not take a large leap to consider that machines, as they pulse electricity and carry out processes, are expending energies, beyond words, enlivening discourse in more-than-human ways. This project aims to continue to explore what it means to think of rhetoric as energy by expanding its scope to account for the energies of lively (but not alive) communication, such as that of computational performances.

By bringing the expenditure and experience of energy in computational performances from the background into the foreground, we can begin to appreciate the something "more" that attends computational performances, or instances of persuasion that leverage the movements of machines. Take, for instance, table 0.1, which compares examples of traditional modes of (human) delivery with computationally performed ones. (Note that the contents of this table also track with the case studies of the book.) The Twitter bot and vaccine web application examples stem from my earlier, less-developed work on "machinic rhetorics."[19] All of the examples in the table are mapped over what Leah Ceccarelli has articulated as the "ends" of rhetoric: the aesthetic, the political, and the epistemic. Important to note is that focusing on the rhetorical energy of machines is to take up concern for the ontological as it regards these three ends of rhetoric.[20] While machines might not be persons engaging in symbolic interaction with other humans, they might nonetheless add something persuasive as machines, located not in stylistics or lines of argument per se, but rather in the energies that attend the performance of computing "at work" as they carry out processes (like calculating and/or lampooning a president).

The idea that machines can add something to rhetoric can be difficult for some people to accept. Helping us understand this is Carolyn Miller, who, in her 2007 study of the rhetorical abilities and effects of machines, shared a description of a fictional speech grading system—replete with the catchy name, AutoSpeech-Easy—with other teachers of rhetoric.[21] Miller's hypothetical AutoSpeech-Easy is described as being able to track not just the language of students' speeches, but also their nonverbal movements and intonations—the energies of their performances. Miller, in her proposition of the hypothetical technology, clairvoyantly projects the robust and steadfast developments of such technologies as facial recognition, motion mapping, and sentiment analysis, at a time in which these technologies were only reaching viable marketability. The fact that these technologies are ubiquitous today underscores the power and durability of her contribution. Based on survey responses from teachers who were asked to consider the use of the technology to grade student speeches, Miller notes a qualitative uneasiness in their reactions having to do with the reluctance to attribute agency to computers. In particular, she notes that the act of "speaking strongly resists automation because we understand it intuitively . . . as a *performance,* meaning that it is dynamic and temporal, that it requires *living* presence."[22] Furthermore, for the respondents, speaking to AutoSpeech-Easy as opposed to a human audience creates a communicative action vacant of "an Other, someone who may resist, disagree, disapprove, humiliate—or approve, appreciate, empathize, and applaud"—it is devoid of the necessary sharing of connection and relational-being-together between living agents.[23]

TABLE 0.1. Traditional and Computational Performances

RHETORICAL ENDS	"TRADITIONALLY" PERFORMED	COMPUTATIONALLY PERFORMED
EPISTEMIC ARGUMENT	A brochure that details the aluminum contents of various vaccines	A web application, styled in the likeness of an "expert" system, which invites input from the user to detail the aluminum contents of various vaccines
AESTHETIC EXPERIENCE	A poetry project, which sources US Census data to tell vivid stories of persons, published in a book	A Twitter bot that will run for the next 1,700 years, sharing a biographical statement for a real person every hour on the hour
POLITICAL CRITIQUE	Alec Baldwin's parody of Donald Trump on *Saturday Night Live*	An autonomous machine-learning system, trained on Donald Trump's public speaking transcripts to perform his "persona"

Miller counters with the suggestion that machines can (and perhaps should) be conceptualized as rhetorical agents at least insofar as they might represent imitations that can invite attributions of (human) agency. Specifically, she notes

9 Introduction

that rhetorical agency exists "exactly between the agent's capacity and the effect on an audience" in what she designates as the "kinetic energy of rhetorical performance."[24] If machines can perform like humans then, by consequence, they can also invite the attribution of agency, represented by the kinetic energies of their rhetorical performances. By kinetic energies, she means the potential energies associated with habits of mind and being that we attribute to human behavior and expectation, scripted, animated, put into motion. Because the movements of machines can instantiate performances of living (just like people do), their status as rhetorical agents is illuminated. But as Miller is careful to note, "we understand agency as an attribution made by another agent, that is, by an entity to whom we are willing to attribute agency. It is through this process of mutual attribution that agency does, indeed, produce the agent."[25] Consequently, she concludes: "Do we owe such acknowledgment, such agency-granting attribution, to automated assessment systems? Right now, I suspect that most of us agree that we do not, and moreover that out of respect for our students we should not ask them to make such attributions either."[26] To use AutoSpeech-Easy to grade student speeches, moreover, would be to revoke the attribution of agency—both as capacity and effect—from the students asked to speak to it, by omitting the something more found in the relations between persons: the emergence of one's own, and others', agency through mutual attribution. Consequently, Miller demonstrates that although machines might be able to perform the kinetic energies of humans, they nonetheless are not alive, and so we might harbor a reluctance to attribute agency to them—either as effect or capacity.

But even if we are reluctant to attribute agency to machines, they continue to impact our interconnected, increasingly automated discourse ecologies.[27] While machines may not be alive, they nonetheless participate in communication, whether or not we grant them agency. Krista Kennedy makes this point through archival examination of Wikipedia articles while shedding light on the machines that human actors collaborate with to compose content on the Wiki platform.[28] Namely, she poignantly describes the compositional process of writing articles about small towns, which in traditional encyclopedic writing were often omitted due to labor constraints. However, with the development of bots, such as Rambot (named after its creator, Derek Ramsey), a software-based agent that sourced raw US Census data to write thousands of articles a day about small towns, we find an impact on the very compositional trajectory of Wikipedia. From there, humans (and other bots) could interact with those articles, adding their contributions and revisions, exposing that even if we refuse to attribute agency to machines, they nonetheless plug away, performing the work of writing. And this is exactly Kennedy's point: By studying the compositional processes of Wikipedia articles, she teaches us that writing, an activity that we often wish to attribute to humans, is something that emerges between the human and the machine. Kennedy explains: "These bots react to their environment, initiate action with it, and affect change both within the texts and sometimes within the broader scope of the project, as when Wikipedia rather suddenly expanded exponentially to cover thousands of towns."[29]

The power of Kennedy's contribution is that even if we refuse to attribute agency to machines, they nonetheless continue to generate articles and police the writing of other authors—they are members of the discourse ecology from which the genre of Wikipedia articles emerges. Surely, creation is an enterprise that we wish to attribute to human ingenuity, but Wikipedia is a creation that would not exist as it does today without the contributions of its bots. The reality of this is that, as much as we might be reluctant to acknowledge it, humans are not the only ones "choosing the right words." Furthermore, and as this book hopes to show, the performances of computing machines also instantiate suasions that go beyond words, for they are attended by *rhetorical energies*—movements and processes that speak beyond words and from beyond the human.

Scaffolding our understanding of rhetorical energies as occurring between humans and nonhumans is Debra Hawhee, whose *Rhetoric in Tooth and Claw* offers a virtuoso reading of classical rhetorical texts, informed by George Kennedy's rhetorical energy. Specifically, she zeros in on (non)human animals as they appear in discussions of language to draw out the relationship between language and sensation. "The snapping of the curs, the crying children, the rushing lion, the leaping puppies," Hawhee says, "are all doing something with intensity of feeling; they embody and convey *pathos*, and that embodiment constitutes their likeness to the human animals being described."[30] Hawhee tracks the distinction that Aristotle makes in *De Anima* between *dunamis* (potential energy) and *energeia* (kinetic energy) into his *Rhetoric*. For Aristotle, she maintains, the invocation of movement—kinetic energy—is what elevates metaphors from the level of a thought to an experience, a "bringing before the eyes."[31] Animals, and especially nonhuman animals, bring "more" than just ideas to language: they bring energy, which activates the body, adding sensation, exposing the abilities of animals to "enliven the imagination."[32] Rather than using metaphors to designate the movements of humans, these metaphors draw on the embodied experience of animal movement, further supporting

11 Introduction

the claim that the rhetorical energies of nonhumans can be leveraged to communicate in ways that go beyond the human. Where the moving snarls of tigers or the quiet hops of rabbits are instances in which the energies of nonhumans elevate lingual metaphors to the status of bringing "more," computing machines similarly add sensations. And surely this can happen in lingual constructions that draw on the movements of machines. For instance, "processing," or even a joking, "error 404, file not found," when a colleague asks when the next meeting is scheduled, are metaphors that imbue the energies of computing machines. However, computational media—web and mobile applications, bots, video games, voice-based assistants—are unique in that they are distinctly characterized by energies of dynamic movement across the senses. Their performances are not moored solely in the verbal, or the visual, but also in sound and touch—they are multisensorial.

One's phone, buzzing in their pocket, alongside a cleverly designed ding is a case in point: the energies of computing machines move across sensory media, finding expression in other senses beyond sight, such as touch and sound. Casey Boyle, James J. Brown, and Steph Ceraso offer the metaphor of transduction to conceptualize an approach to rhetoric that is willing to explore not sight, or any other single sense, but rather the multiplicity of senses that span a wide sector of the digital sensorium that characterizes daily life. In their words: "Transduction refers to how a signal moves across disparate registers of relations: neural firings move to fingers to perform keystrokes that then transform into electrical charges that then become digital bits and are delivered to a screen by software or saved to a hard drive that becomes transcoded again whenever someone opens a file."[33] Accounting for the multiplicity of energies of a given computational performance, manifested as converging and diverging light, sound, and/or physical movement, is a means for accounting for the digital sensorium; not individual visuals added to sounds and touches, but rather as a more holistic energy that attends the convergence of those stimuli transduced (converted) into the body. As multisensorial complexes of movement, the performances of computing machines, while not alive, can be approached as lively.

To regard computing machines as lively, rather than alive, is to recognize that computing machines do not enact agency in the sense of an invested "mind" influencing another. However, they are attended by energies in the form of movements entangled with the concerns of humans, animating communication in distinctly nonhuman, nonverbal, and visceral ways. For example, as I have written about elsewhere, the "steam engine," as it bellowed steam and moved rods, "echoed the spirit of science, come to save us from our human shortcomings," and the flipping of switches and the flashing of neon bulbs of early computers moved with the reassuring (alarming?) character of "mechanical Frankenstein's monsters, birthed from the work of groups of mathematicians, scientists, and engineers recurrently visiting a problem in order to systematically remove the human from the idea in order to inscribe it into the program of a given circuit."[34] Approaches to rhetorical agency that orient toward humans, and words, and arguments will surely find these things in computing machines. However, such approaches also problematically overlook those instances of impact that move beyond human control, verbal articulation, and argumentative rationality, wherein the energies transduced are not merely artificial or natural—they are an amalgamation of both. People make computing machines, but computing machines move on their own.

To approach the agency of computing machines this way is to follow Karen Barad in taking up an agential realist approach, which recognizes that mattering (in the sense of making meaningful) and matter (in the sense of the stuff of physics) are entangled with respect to agential outcomes.[35] The feelings and ideas of humans, moreover, are not the results of direct human action, but rather the results of intra-actions between humans and nonhumans, and even nonhumans and nonhumans, including matter, catalyzing outcomes.[36] Within this framing, rather than look only for the interactions between a human and another human, mediated by a chatbot, for instance, one can also look for the intra-actions in which the chatbot emerges as an active participant, attended by catalyzing energies. A chatbot may be made by a person. But a chatbot moves on its own, representing not just the (human) preprogrammed joke that "Pineapple does not belong on pizza," but also the (machinic) movement of code—the energy of mathematics incarnate—a human concern, expressed in a more-than-human way. The mattering of matter in the chatbot, put differently, is not merely the outcome of thoughtful, eloquent humans; the chatbot is also moving.

Accounting for the energies that attend computing machines is to enact what Barad calls a posthuman approach to performativity—not meant to reject human impact, but rather to add nuance to how mattering is negotiated between bodies (human and nonhuman).[37] Particularly productive is Barad's advice to focus on performance, rather than words, as a means for capturing the impacts of the nonhuman. As Krista Kennedy succinctly articulates: "Conceptualized as performance rather than as inherent capacity, agency is not a property that a subject can possess . . . but rather it arises through response to a situation composed of parameters beyond the control of any single actor."[38]

13 Introduction

That is, rather than focus solely on the salty and sweet words of the chatbot, a rhetoric as energy approach to computing machines would pay particular attention to the sorts of intra-actions of energy taking place in the performance of the chatbot as it draws on traditions of chatbot design and electricity to move according to its scripts, illuminates pixels, and chimes with "Bleebloop" sounds. While machines may not be invested minds, making appeals to others, they do instantiate performances, intermingling in the wider discourse ecology, moving on their own, reacting to situations, imbuing them with energies.

To explore the rhetorical energy of machines, then, is to drive at the multisensory, visceral "more" that attends computational performances. Rhetoric as energy does not necessarily displace verbal eloquence or logical rationality. Those aspects of rhetoric remain. However, in conceptualizing rhetoric as energy, one's focus of analysis is made broader, zooming out to account for the background feelings and visceral responses of bodies to sensory stimuli, which might be hidden in ambience, but nonetheless are moving (both in the sense of physical movement and in the sense of impacting bodies). We need to be willing to go deeper than asking how machines may, or may not, mime humans, and take seriously the idea that, despite being nonhuman and nonanimal, they also bring lively movements as machines.

Beyond the Front and the Back Ends of Computing and Toward the Deep End

In computing, there are two general realms, divided by a metaphoric expression describing that which is visible and that which is hidden from view.

The front end: The realm of computing that deals with the user interface (i.e., recieving input and giving output).

The back end: The realm of computing that deals with the databases, functions, and networking from which a given program operates (i.e., information processing and storage).

However, there is another end of computing—buried in ambience—existing as an intertextual flurry of cultural beliefs, affects, and practices, where the entanglements of feeling and culture are catalyzed by the energies of computational performances.

The deep end: The realm of computing that deals with the performative expenditure and experience of machinic rhetorical energies (i.e., the catalyzing of visceral feelings).

14 Influential Machines

Orienting to the deep end is to point attention to the energies that animate computational performances manifest not in the front end or the back end alone, but between them, as they are entangled with wider ecologies of discourse. The deep end of computing is characterized by enculturated habits of response regarding nature and artifice, *Terminator,* patriarchy, neural networks, tropes of prophets and seers, software ecologies, and the material compositions of networks; happenings, tropes, and material realities that ambiently shape the animating energies of machines. The overlooking of the deep end is, at least partially, supported by what David Gunkel would point out is an apparent effort to cling to the notion that computing machines are merely media of human communication, rather than communicators themselves.[39] It is for precisely this reason that pursuing the deep end is a critical move for understanding the suasions of machines, for they increasingly govern expression,[40] perpetuate stereotypical representations of marginalized identities,[41] and even take on the characters of "racist sociopath[s]."[42] As such, we must understand the rhetorical energies that attend their performances by diving deep into the ecologies that animate them.

To dive into the deep end requires tacking back and forth between the front and back ends of a given computational performance, discovering connections between its sensory output and background processes to "thicken" an understanding of its energies.[43] Throughout the case studies of this book, I explore the gap between the front and the back ends not only by analyzing the user interfaces of machinic performances, but also the procedures that drive and characterize them. In some cases, where it is accessible, I also incorporate "readings" of code from the back end with my analyses of front-end output. To tack back and forth between the back end and the front end is a move toward what Annette Vee has identified as "full stack rhetoric" or scholarship that explores rhetorics between the front and the back end, for both the front and back ends are part and parcel of the enterprise of computing.[44] The energies of computational performances are not simply expended when they render "outputs" on the front end. They are also expended in the processes of the machine as it evaluates variables and loops through conditional states on the back end. Consequently, a full stack rhetoric—a rhetoric concerned with both the front and the back ends—is required for thickening understanding of the deep ends that animate the energies of machines, fore-fronting the ambient environs from which they emerge.

The deep end of computing is an ambient rhetoric, which Thomas Rickert articulates as being located in the *chora*—the place—from which rhetorical action and thinking emerges. Locating rhetoric this way dethrones the rational

15 Introduction

human subject as manipulator of nature and instead redistributes agency across an ecology of actants, interconnected by ambient ideas and processes.[45] Put in terms of an allegory that Rickert uses at the outset of his *Ambient Rhetoric,* the impactful character of a wine does not emerge solely from the hand of the vintner; it is also a matter of the soil, the grapes, and the stories of the land from which they grow, fermenting impact on the embodied mind. The character of the wine is as much a product of the environment as it is the human who processed the grapes. Such a reorientation to rhetoric expands the scope of rhetoric beyond words, beyond human actors, and beyond isolated "situations," urging the analyst to dig deeper into the otherwise invisible substrate of rhetorical processes, covered over with human hubris, forgetfulness, and shortsighted yearnings to uphold the superiority of rationality.

We gain valuable insight when we adjust the aperture of rhetorical scholarship in ways that flatten and bring into focus the background with which embodied minds and things are entangled. In the specific case of machine communication, importing the *chora* of computing—its ambiance of ideas, wires, codes, networks, interfaces, and bodies—allows for tacking back and forth between the front end and back end, pushing us toward the deep end that animates the rhetorical energies of computational performance. Orienting oneself to the deep end of computing is to orient to the conditions that shape the energies of machines as they run conditional loops and evaluate variables on the back end, expressing output on the front end.

Particularly useful for approaching the feelings that attend the rhetorical energies of machines, as they are steeped in ambience, is Rickert's operationalization of Martin Heidegger's concept of *Stimmung*—"attunement" (sometimes translated as "mood").[46] While it can be frustrating to pin down consistent definitions of just what scholars mean when they are using terms to talk about feelings and sensations, here I borrow from Rickert's explanation to define some important terms to help in clarifying what attunement is. Broadly speaking, one can conceptualize a distinction between emotions and moods. *Emotions* are specific, articulable, states (e.g., happiness, anger, sadness, surprise, fear). *Moods,* on the other hand, are more general (often longer lasting), vaguer states (e.g., contentedness or angst). While moods do not necessitate specific emotional states, moods do impact the range of emotional possibility. Anyone who has awoken in an angsty mood, for instance, might note that, while it is not impossible to be happy, it is nonetheless harder to be. And, conversely, waking in a contented mood one might find it harder to be angry, but easier to be happy. One's moods impact how they emerge into the world. This tracks with what Heidegger means by attunement, only his account is more robust in its recognition that one's feelings in the world are not constituted merely of emotional content, but also lifeworld content. Ideas, assumptions, feelings, culture, previous experience—they shape, and are shaped by, our feelings. Thus, attunement is a means of catching glimpses at those affects that precede cognition, constituting our being-in-the-world, shaped by that which is beyond, but also within, the body. In this sense, when we are speaking of the deep end of computing, we are not attempting to name the specific emotional states invoked by the energies of computational performances. We are, however, attempting to dive deep into their ambient conditions to explain the possibilities of attunement that attend the energies of those performances.

Where some modernist visions of rhetoric might locate emotion as secondary to logic, approaching feelings as something added to arguments, Heidegger posits that emotion is more constitutive. According to Daniel Gross, Heidegger's positioning of feelings as prior to logic places emphasis on the necessary energies implied in rhetorical action, for "without affect our disembodied minds would have no heart, and no legs to stand on. We would have no grounds for concern, no time and place for judging, no motivation to discourse at all."[47] As such, attunements are mishmashes of feelings and logical content (e.g., "I feel like something is incorrect here."). Feeling is primary to, but nonetheless refracted by, logic.

Heidegger's attunement, moreover, helps us recognize that messy estuary between sensation and cognition, wherein a piece of music does not simply afford a sad state but also is attended by an anxious attunement (which also feels like being in space, hurtling through a galaxy), informed by our cultural experiences with analog synthesizer sounds, cinema, and fast, erratically paced syncopation. Heidegger's attunement is an answer to the problem that Hawhee raises concerning rhetorical scholarship of sensation—those processes by which bodies take up stimuli through the senses: "How to write about sensation without positing an individual as opposed to a collective, or of thinking in terms of communal sensation, without presuming sameness?"[48] Attunement affords terminology for the analyst to orient to the feelings / logics that attend a given energy without falling into the trap of attempting to declare the specific emotional states or sensations experienced by persons or that all persons within a given public are the same. Instead of assessing feelings as happy or sad, attunement involves an orientation to the general states of affect that attend a given set of energies, not as individually experienced emotion, but rather as communal mood, while at the same time, bearing recognition that it is analytically

17 Introduction

productive to approach feeling and logic as entangled with one another. Where feeling can absolutely be conceived as something distinct from (and perhaps less than) logic, or that it is merely an individually experienced phenomenon, Heidegger's attunement captures the fact that we are social animals that emerge into the world through culturally shaped bodies that both exert and experience energies, physical and emotional, including those of nonhumans.

Byron Hawk helps us navigate the complex of nonhuman and human energies. In his essay on the keyword of *resonance* in the context of sonic rhetorics, he forwards a materialist approach to rhetoric with a penchant for the transduction of energy. In his words: "Bodies are entangled through circulatory waves of energy and force, where resonance layers and amplifies multiple vibrations and sustains them up through knowledge production and cultural circulation."[49] Particularly helpful here is breaking apart *energy* and *force* as they are construed in the process of resonance. Energy is the thing that is "at work"—light or motion, for instance—whereas force is the vibratory resonance of that energy on some other thing(s), such as a person. Catherine Chaput's "affective energies" approach makes a similar distinction between "affect" (which in her frame is equated with energy) and "sensation" (the apprehension of energy by the body), which positions "emotion" as the conscious rationalization of a given sensation.[50] Chaput is largely concerned with human rhetorical energies, which makes sense, given that she is developing affective energies in the context of human systems of labor and capital.

By contrast, the current inquiry is interested in the energies contributed by computational performances—lively, but nonhuman, machinic energies. Furthermore, distinguishing between energy and force (breaking matters "at work" apart from the resonant moods that attend them) clears space for the energies of nonhumans to be acknowledged as they contribute to the cultivation of attunements. This is what Rickert means when he says that "rhetoric is not . . . energy, per se, but rather a need and a capacity in relation to the world and other entities that has to be discovered and deployed," a view that resonates with Annette Vee and James J. Brown, in their brief connection to rhetorical energy in the introduction to the "Rhetoric and Computation" special issue of *Computational Culture;* they note that rhetorical energy "is not primarily about meaning but is rather that which triggers discourse."[51] Rhetorical force does not exist in the energies of machinic performances or discourse alone, it exists in the animating resonances between them.

Computational performances emerge as nodal bursts of energy, which we might deny or confuse either as "just the way it is," or a simple trick, "making

18 Influential Machines

us believe it is an animal," overlooking that they nonetheless affect us, encouraging attunements as machines. To analyze the deep end of computing is to mobilize Rickert's ambient rhetoric, by accounting for the lively energies of computational performances as well as the antecedents of discourse that shape them. As the case studies in this book illustrate, the machinic energies of computational performances can cultivate attunements of contentedness or angst. But before moving into the case studies, it is important to first articulate what is added by *rhetorical energy* as a term of art in rhetorical analysis of computing by discussing it in relation to what many would identify as the defining rhetorical characteristic of computational media: procedurality.

Thickening Procedurality with the Rhetorical Energies of Computational Performance

"Procedural rhetoric," as Ian Bogost first articulates the idea in his *Persuasive Games,* "is a technique for making arguments with computational systems and for unpacking computational arguments others have created."[52] Video games, for instance, can invite users to take on a particular worldview by way of presenting decisions and giving feedback on those decisions (e.g., being "rewarded" with forward progress by exploiting natural resources to "craft" a more lovely island). Such is an argument moored squarely in an interactive experience, which encourages the player to accept a conclusion not stated through verbal claims and evidence but rather through decision trees.

Although Bogost tends to favor video games as his examples of procedural rhetoric, James J. Brown is quick to note that procedural rhetoric is applicable to the broader realm of software while making the extended point that rhetorical outcomes are mutually shaped between people and machines amid networked technologies, resulting in discourses that demonstrate "the predicament of hospitality" in that proceduralization cannot open to a habit of being without closing off from, or constraining, other habits of being.[53]

> Procedural arguments involve explicit statements ("If X, then do Y"), but this does not mean that the arguments themselves are explicit. Like an enthymeme that omits one of its premises, a procedural argument has embedded assumptions, and this invites the audience to interact and interpret. Engaging with a procedural argument involves more than reading content—it involves reading the rules that generate that content and understanding how those rules express certain worldviews. Further, procedural arguments simultaneously insist on the execution of

19 Introduction

sets of instructions and invite interaction with those instructions. Once again, we are presented with the predicament of hospitality—procedural rhetoric both invites interaction and attempts to hold it at a distance.[54]

Kevin Brock and Dawn Shepherd extend this line of thinking in what they coin as "procedural enthymemes," or logical structures in software, which encourage users to infer conclusions from the premises implied in the operation of a program as it "analyzes potential connections across multiple points of data to 'understand' particular subjects."[55] Carbon footprint software, which encourages the user to conclude that they need to change their daily recycling habits, based on the premise that the software's analysis has discovered a negative impact on the environment from the user's inputs, would be an example of a procedural enthymeme. At the outset of their article, Brock and Shepherd draw a passing connection between rhetorical energy and computing machines, wherein they cite Kennedy's "Hoot in the Dark" to clear space for nonhumans—such as algorithms—to be considered as rhetorical. While Brock and Shepherd are more interested in articulating the premises of argument that exist in a given software than they are in the energies of lively machinic performances, their connection to Kennedy is generative in the sense of moving toward the computational machine not merely as a medium of arguments (as in the decision trees of video games), but as a performer of arguments (as in the performance of "data analysis"). Put differently, Brock and Shepherd's work puts us on a path to recognizing that the movement—the energy—of the machine is just as important to its influence as the line of argument that it represents.

For example, in the case of a carbon footprint calculator, the front end might be adorned by clever graphic designs and user-interface elements that allow one to indicate details such as how many people live in their household and whether they drive a car. Those elements may convey the generally "busy" aesthetic of a scientific organization, wherein, alongside the user-interface elements, text blobs explain the methodologies used to design the application. Procedurally, the user is asked to share their daily behaviors by entering numbers of miles driven in a car or flown in an airplane, offering a logic that directly ties one's personal behaviors to environmental impact. The user can even play with the numbers, demonstrating variance in their carbon output, which reifies the notion that even small changes in one's daily living can have concrete impacts on climate change, based on scripts operating on the back end of the application.

20   Influential Machines

But if we articulate the rhetorical energies of the carbon footprint application, we discover "more." In particular, as the case study of the first chapter will elaborate in more detail, within the deep end of computing exists the trope of the prophet as well as the rituals of interaction endemic to expert systems, which can afford an attunement, wherein the user is encouraged to feel that the conclusions of the application are true, realized not just in the procedures the user is asked to interact with, but also in the performance of "running calculations," enlivening an argument about environmental relations amid the Anthropocene, by leveraging the energies of a computing machine to speak to human concerns in a more-than-human way. The application is attended by a feeling just as much as it instantiates an argument, explainable not simply by way of the front or back end, but rather by diving into the deep end of computing, where longstanding discourses (like those of oracles and rituals of expert systems) ambiently shape, and are shaped by, the movements evident in the front and the back end processes—the energies—of the performance.

Surely the procedural argument of the carbon footprint calculator is integral to its influence, but much in the same way that the prosody of one's voice is integral to the force of their articulations of reason so too is rhetorical energy to the procedures of computational performances (see table 0.2). And those energies impact the culturally shaped body to animate attunements, comportments of feeling. Casey Boyle, drawing on Jeffrey Walker's classical rhetorical work, notes that despite common assumptions about classical rhetoric, which might imagine that enthymemes deal simply in logic and meaning, they also deal in emotion. And if we take such a realization a step further to focus on rhetorical practice from a posthumanist perspective, we will see that enthymemes are better understood not as "missing" a conclusion to be filled in by an audience, but rather as nodal flashpoints, where pre-existing ideas and feelings are transduced from a complex of practices, tied together by an ever-evolving ecology of objects, including humans.[56] The carbon footprint calculator may very well instantiate an argument, manifest as a procedural enthymeme. But the carbon footprint calculator also instantiates a performance, manifest as "running the numbers." Consequently, its effect is not simply meaning or logic changing one's mind: it is also an attunement, catalyzed from the energies of machinic movement, resonating with existing discourses of the prophet and expert systems to animate an embodied consideration of the relationship between daily practices and CO_2 output.

We experience the rhetorical energies of computational performance in ways that we are unaccustomed to naming, for they exist beyond the paradigm

TABLE 0.2. Distinctions Between Procedurality and Rhetorical Energies in an Analysis of a Carbon Footprint Calculator

PROCEDURE	ARGUMENT(S)	ENERGY	DEEP END	ATTUNEMENT
If the carbon footprint is greater than X, suggest Y behavior	One's behavior matters to the environment Changing one's individual behavior can have a desirable impact on CO2 numbers	The performance of information analysis and retrieval	The rituals of interaction, endemic to the tradition of expert systems, manifest in the front and back ends of the application, further resonating with the trope of the prophet (wherein an agent interprets truth directly from the ether)	Contentedness

of rhetoric as the enterprise of influence had between humans as symbol-using animals.[57] Humans obviously use symbols; but we also feel in the world, and, at least some of the time, we are affected by nonhumans, who may not influence us as invested minds making appeals to us, but who absolutely influence us at the level of conveying lively rhetorical energies that interact with our culturally shaped bodies. Brown, in his reflective response to the essays of *Rhetorical Machines: Writing, Code, and Computational Ethics,* makes a nod to the shortcomings of logocentric rhetorical scholarship of computing, noting that "like any symbol system, code will always elude our grasp, and digital rhetoricians' move along a continuum from rhetoric (back?) to logic may put us at risk of forgetting this."[58]

Similarly, outside of rhetorical studies, in the realm of human–machine communication, where scholarship is largely quantitative (rather than interpretive), one of the earliest leaders of the field, Steve Jones, has identified "context" as well as "symbolic and affective dimensions" as integral to accounting for the communication between humans and machines.[59] This book is an attempt to move toward a necessary thickening of the idea of procedural rhetoric, which locates not just the arguments and logics of software, but also its sensations and feelings, offering an interpretive framework useful for accounting for the deeper contexts from which the affective influence of computing machines emerge.

In subsequent chapters, I argue that the movements of a web application can imbibe the prophetic energy of an all-seeing oracle, a Twitterbot can radiate the sublime energy of nature, and machine-learning systems can signal the "purity" of mathematics. I will also demonstrate that taking seriously the influential energies of computational performance requires revisiting long-standing assumptions about communication ethics, which might problematically define responsibility in terms of the living, and not the lively, resulting in designs of machine communication that do not adequately "hedge bets" against moments in which the machine might catalyze negative energies, beyond the intentions of designers.

It is important to note that the goal of this book is to equip readers with concepts useful for analyzing and thinking through computational performance, even if the technologies of computational performance might be evolving rapidly. That is, while the web applications, bots, and voice assistants discussed in this book might reach a state of technological obsolescence, the concepts built from studying them establish a working foundation from which to integrate, and adapt to, shifts in the technological landscape. This book is about pushing rhetoric to put us on a path toward grappling with computational performance, even if, by its very nature, computational media will likely evolve beyond the scope of the individual case studies discussed herein.

The chapters of the book are organized around what Leah Ceccarelli has articulated as the three ends of rhetoric: the epistemic, the aesthetic, and the political.[60] The first case study focuses on the manufactured processing of a simple web application designed by vaccine denialists. The second case study interrogates the processual magnitude of a piece of data art. And the third case study examines the processual signaling of a neural-net-based political performance.

Beyond organization around science, art, and politics, the reader will also notice that the objects of each case study increase in complexity and range of autonomous movement to further illustrate that, while entangled with procedures, computational performances do not necessarily require interaction in the sense of a user or player making choices through a decision tree. The web application of the first case is bound to user interaction. But the bots in the second and third case studies do not require user interaction to carry out their processes—they are, to use the parlance of rhetoric, more monologic than dialogic. Further, this sequencing also tracks with increasing autonomy on the part of the machines. The web application of the first case moves only in response to user interaction. The bot of the second case autonomously generates messaging within the constraints of pre-programmed parameters independently of user interaction. And the neural network of the third case autonomously generates messaging with much looser constraints imposed by the programmer without requiring user interaction.

Following the case studies is a meditation on ethical critique and design of computational performances with concern for the good or ill that computational performances can imbue to the social ecology with their lively (but not alive) movements. The book concludes with a discussion of the value of a rhetoric as energy approach to the growing field of human–machine communication by examining the lively movements of machine communicators amid the COVID-19 pandemic. For now, to further parse the rhetorical energies of computing machines from the procedures that punctuate them, I examine the prophetic energies of Vaccine Calculator.

1

Manufactured Processing, Ritual, and Expert Systems

Douglas Adams, in *The Hitchhiker's Guide to the Galaxy*, describes Deep Thought, an all-knowing computer that has spent 7.5 million years calculating the answer to the great question "of Life, the Universe, and Everything."[1] When asked for the answer, Deep Thought replies, much to the hilarious delight of the reader: "Forty-two."[2] The joke, like many of Adams's, operates by drawing attention to a category mistake, revealed in a seemingly random, capricious conclusion made by an entity from whom the reader is primed to expect a reasoned, sensible answer. Beyond bringing some levity, Deep Thought's answer is also productive in that it reminds us that automated machines are a special class of agent associated with expectations of correctness and nontriviality. Such an *ethos* can be leveraged for humorous ends (as Adams does in his fiction). But the energies of computational performance can also be leveraged outside of fiction and in ways far less humorous. Here in this chapter, I pursue a case of *manufactured processing* or the tactic of leveraging computational performance to construct legitimacy for claims that are not defensible with respect to overwhelming scientific consensus.[3]

In the same way that including an unnecessary graph or formula can bolster scientific persuasiveness, the tactic of marshaling computational performance to argue on one's behalf can be used by counterpublics of science to garner legitimacy for pseudoscientific claims. Manufactured processing is a particularly dangerous tactic in science contexts because it can encourage users who lack understanding to nonetheless feel like experts, working in collaboration with machinic agents normally associated with legitimate science. This chapter expounds the idea of manufactured processing in an analysis of Vaccine Calculator, a web application designed by vaccine denialists to perform as an "expert" system, which functions rhetorically by cultivating a sense of

25 Manufactured Processing, Ritual, and Expert Systems

contentedness, enlivened by the movements of an automated agent, emergent from a deep end of computing shaped by rituals of legitimate health science and entangled with the trope of the prophet. To fully appreciate what is alarming about the rhetorical energies of Vaccine Calculator, it is essential to first discuss science signaling and its relationship to the performances of machinic agents, punctuated by rituals of science and shaped by genre ecologies of knowledge-based systems.

Automation as Ritual of Science

Aping particular forms of science communication can have potent effects on the persuasiveness of claims about health. Quantification, for example, can offer the effect of appearing more factual by rendering content into numbers.[4] Similarly, including trivial charts and graphs can add persuasiveness to truth claims.[5] In a study run by Aner Tal and Brian Wansink, sixty-one people were given the same information about a fictional drug designed to reduce susceptibility to the common cold.[6] The researchers split participants into two groups. One group got the original text, and the other group got the original text plus a graph that reiterated some of the text in a visual aid. That is, the text told the participants that colds occurred in nearly 90 percent of people who did not take the fictional drug, compared to just under 50 percent in people who took the drug. In the graph condition, the visual aid merely reiterated those numbers. With posttest survey data, the authors found that "while only two thirds of the people believed the medication would reduce illness without the graph, all but one participant in the graphs condition believed this."[7] After replicating the study with fifty-six participants to control for possible repetition effects on information understanding and retention, the authors also found that persons with stronger beliefs in science were those who demonstrated the most considerable effect when the graph was present. In a third study of fifty-seven persons, the authors gave each participant a description of a fictional drug, which is "carbon-oxygen-helium and-fluorine based," but gave only one half the chemical formula: "$C_{21}H_{29}FO_5$."[8] Similar to the first two studies, participants in the formula condition reported more confidence in the drug. Despite the graphs and the formula being unnecessary for communicating the drugs' effectiveness or composition, the inclusion of such trivial elements increased the confidence of study participants. In their conclusions, Tal and Wansink compellingly describe the effects of including trivial components in one's science communication as science "signaling," which works by playing off of elements—like graphs and formulas—to associate claims made with scientific objectivity, in turn, augmenting the authority of those claims.

In the context of automation, making one's argument "move" by retrieving data and returning calculations to a user, in other words, can be done trivially, and, as I will demonstrate in the case of Vaccine Calculator, machines can perform as agents of legitimate science and public health, but without actually being a part of those spheres. In such cases, the machinic agent instantiates a manufacturing of legitimacy by way of emulating the rituals of interface one might commonly associate with scientific expertise, enlivened by the rhetorical energies of computational performance.

Theorization about visual rhetorics of science and technology offers a useful proxy for adding depth to understanding manufactured processing—namely, its implications for enhancing ethos through ritual. Lynda Walsh, in her *Scientists as Prophets: A Rhetorical Genealogy*, illustrates the "prophetic *ethos*" that attends climate model visualizations. In Walsh's frame, worn into the grooves of historical trajectory, since the days of the Greeks, we have looked to "oracles" to see the truth—even in science.[9] Within the mimetically repeated trope of the prophet, there are also technologies of prophecy, such as climate model visualizations, which help to discern the ether of data and dynamism that constitutes climate change. It is in this way that climate change modeling plays off of the longstanding trope of the prophetic ethos. When we look at a climate model, we are looking at the work of seers, reporting back, after they have "read the bones."

Within this frame, we can grasp that computational performances represent "more" than just the data; they instantiate the animation of ecologies of ideas, shaped by practices and habits entangled with historical echoes of expectation that still resonate with practices of science, like the trope of the prophet as it resonates with the automation of data retrieval and analysis. To further account for the deep end of computing that matters to the case of Vaccine Calculator, I will take up what Clay Spinuzzi has articulated as *interface archaeology*.[10] In this analytic approach, one dives into the meanings and effects of a given interface, by retracing the evolutions of similar interfaces by locating antecedents of cultural practice within, and around, those interfaces. For example, analyzing a geographic mapping interface not simply by focusing on the interface itself, but also by accounting for the genre ecology that matters to that interface (e.g., by looking to historical designs of mapping interfaces and how they have evolved over time, in step with other technologies that preceded them, like colored pins or paper maps).[11]

27 Manufactured Processing, Ritual, and Expert Systems

Because the current study is interested in the deep ends of computing—the energies of computational performance, manifest not just in the front end, but between the front and the back ends—I will place attention on the interface of Vaccine Calculator, but also its back-end processes. By doing so, we will be doing not just an interface archaeology, but an archaeology of computational performance, for genres of computational performance are constituted not only by visual representations but also by manners of movement (as in when a machine reacts to input, based on its programming on the back end). Furthermore, I will show that the computational performance of Vaccine Calculator is entangled with cultural practices—rituals—associated with science communication and human–computer interaction, enlivening claims about health science by animating them with machinic movement. Specifically, I will draw attention to the procedures of Vaccine Calculator and how they mime the rituals of legitimate health science while performing as an "expert" system, inviting users to attune to "expert" knowledge with a misplaced contentedness, empowering them to find false legitimacy in pseudoscience. For now, we turn to begin describing some characteristics of the genre ecology of knowledge-based systems.

Knowledge-Based Systems and Looking to Machines for Answers about Health

It takes only a small interaction with Amazon's Alexa, who answers your voice-based query about what the proper name for a group of unicorns is—"A group of unicorns is called a 'blessing'"—or a brief session with IBM's Watson, which, according to its automated sentiment analysis, informs you that your academic writing is low on "joy" but high on "anger," to realize that we look to machines for answers.[12] The disappearance of machine communicators into the background of our everyday assemblages of public life is striking, despite their relatively recent history existing only in practical terms as mockups and props displayed on the soundstages of sci-fi programs, like *Star Trek: The Next Generation*.[13] The resources required to make such machines are minor, especially in contrast to the teams of experts, expensive equipment, and trial and error traditionally necessary to creating such systems.[14] In other words, the genre of software agents that is referred to as *expert systems* is a genre that is increasingly accessible to the wider public, beyond the traditionally exclusive realms of technical action and discourse.

All one requires to create a "knowledge-based" system (sometimes called an "expert system") is a knowledge base (derived from content experts) and an

28 Influential Machines

inference engine (a computer program that follows "scripts" to make use of the content).[15] Although this might appear daunting to some readers, and while it might require some working knowledge of coding, it is important to underscore the ease with which one can make such a system. If someone already has even an entry-level understanding of coding and they were interested to make their own "expert system," they could easily have an inference engine up and running in a couple of hours, after reading a few of articles, watching a YouTube video, and copying and pasting someone else's code (e.g., see Chatterbot below). And, using that, one can design a system to work from any knowledge base, including knowledge bases that are not derived from actual experts. The scripting of a given knowledge-based system can be simple or complex.[16] For example, one could build a more straightforward knowledge-based system with a few simple "conditionals" that simply return values prescribed in a database, but which adjust to inputs (e.g., taking a user's input of "age" and adjusting a vaccine schedule to give suggested dates of vaccination). Or one might build a system that uses machine learning to "discover" and illustrate patterns in a large data set, outputting suggestions for closer inspection by a human user. While knowledge-based systems that employ machine learning can exhibit more complexity, building one is made easier with the use of third-party services (e.g., see IBM's Watson above) which provide pre-built machine learning tasks in an on-demand fashion, without requiring the coder to know how to make their own machine-learning system.

Technically speaking, because knowledge-based systems replicate the thinking and analytic processes of humans, they instantiate artificial intelligence. However, as computer scientists Rajendra A. Akerkar and Priti Srinivas Sajja explain, there are two types of artificial intelligence. Some systems instantiate *symbolic* artificial intelligence—preprogrammed rules designed to emulate human thinking and action in a rigid way.[17] "How much philosophy is too much, as per my body-weight?" There are also systems that use statistical probabilities to map "fuzzy logical" relationships between variables. These would instantiate *connectionist* artificial intelligence. "Computer, can you tell me if this statement is from a person who has had too much philosophy?" It is imperative to acknowledge that, in actual practice, knowledge-based systems are often mixtures of symbolic and connectionist elements.[18] For example, someone could foreseeably "train" a neural network—a connectionist model—on medical textbooks and retrieve information from that database in the case that the preprogrammed rule set for a given response was unable to retrieve an answer. Conversely, one might symbolically preprogram specific responses

29 Manufactured Processing, Ritual, and Expert Systems

that are facilitated by connectionist natural language processing to get the gist of a user's inquiry, retrieving content based within a threshold of confidence (e.g., see Cox's Chatterbot as an example of such a system).[19]

Vaccine Calculator is a pseudoscientific knowledge-based system that can be categorized as a simple instance of symbolic artificial intelligence in that it operates on simple rules, rather than connectionist mathematical models. Because Vaccine Calculator does not exist in a vacuum, but rather as emerging from existing genre ecologies, it is useful to retrace similar web applications as they are used within the spheres of legitimate health science. An example of a web application representing legitimate health science is the Catch-Up Vaccination Scheduler, a first-of-a-kind tool born out of a collaboration between the Centers for Disease Control (CDC) and the Georgia Institute of Technology.[20] The tool was designed to help simplify and streamline the personalization of vaccine scheduling by drawing on current guidelines of vaccination, and automatically coordinating inputs about a particular person, such as age and current vaccine status, to output a schedule of vaccine recommendations for that person.[21] The Catch-Up Scheduler largely instantiates symbolic artificial intelligence in that it involves referencing current data and then sculpting an output of that data based on user input. Take for instance a snippet of the JavaScript program that runs the Catch-Up Scheduler (replete with the programmer's comments embedded within the code, following "//"s). Basically, it describes the retrieval of vaccine data, designated as the variable vdb, and then parses that data so it can be returned to users, based on their inputs.

```
$http.get(vdbFile).then(function(response) {
        var vdb = response.data
//initialize vaccine data list so that we can populate it fresh with data from
the vdb file.
        factory.vaccineDataList = [];
//loop through the vdb json and get the data we need
        Object.keys(vdb).forEach( function(key) {
            var vacJson = {};
            vacJson['vacId'] = vdb[key].id;
            vacJson['vaccine'] = vdb[key].shortName;
            vacJson['description'] = vdb[key].longName;
            vacJson['numDoses'] = vdb[key].doses.length;
            vacJson['vaccineUrl'] = vdb[key].vaccineInfoUrl;
            factory.vaccineDataList.push(vacJson);
```

```
//Only override the vacAdminDates if they do not exist
    if(!(factory.vacAdminDates[vdb[key].id])){
        factory.vacAdminDates[vdb[key].id] = [];
    }
  });
};[22]
```

The Catch-Up Scheduler was designed to help parents and physicians update missed vaccines for both children and adults. The particular sets of data points (e.g., types of recommended vaccines), as well as the processing of those data points as per particular inputs (e.g., the age of a child, which vaccines have already been administered) can be nebulous. As such, the application was designed to help simplify the otherwise complex and potentially overwhelming sets of variables involved in creating a vaccine schedule, which includes timings of vaccination, sequencing of vaccination as well as the possibilities of discretionary movement of those timings and sequencing for a particular patient.[23] Furthermore, the processing of those data points is done in line with rules, garnered from content experts. Specifically, the Catch-Up Vaccination Scheduler has been designed in accordance with the "Childhood and Adolescent Immunization Schedule," derived from deliberations among members of the Advisory Committee on Immunization Practices, The American Academy of Pediatrics, the American Academy of Family Physicians, and the American College of Obstetricians and Gynecologists.[24] Eventually, we will see that the rhetorical strategy of Vaccine Calculator, a similar, but pseudoscientific web application, is to emulate the performance of such an expert system, but independently of mainstream science, offering science ritual without scientific credentials.

For now, we can say that the rhetorical effect of the CDC's Immunization Scheduler is in the fact that it affords agency to users to sidestep the "all at once" anxiety that some experience when it comes to the complicated barrage of variables involved with coordinating vaccine schedules. For instance, some parents are not necessarily dubious about the effectiveness of vaccines, but they might question the health implications regarding how many and at what time to administer a vaccine. The CDC's Immunization Scheduler empowers users to participate in vaccination, offering further clarity, realized through the movements of a computing machine, encouraging a contented attunement to vaccination, wherein the parent is making choices, not about whether they will vaccinate, but rather when and how, by receiving personalized information

31 Manufactured Processing, Ritual, and Expert Systems

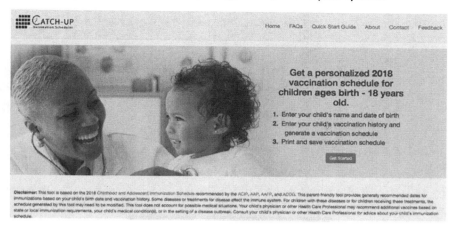

Figure 1.1. CDC Catch-Up Immunization Landing Page

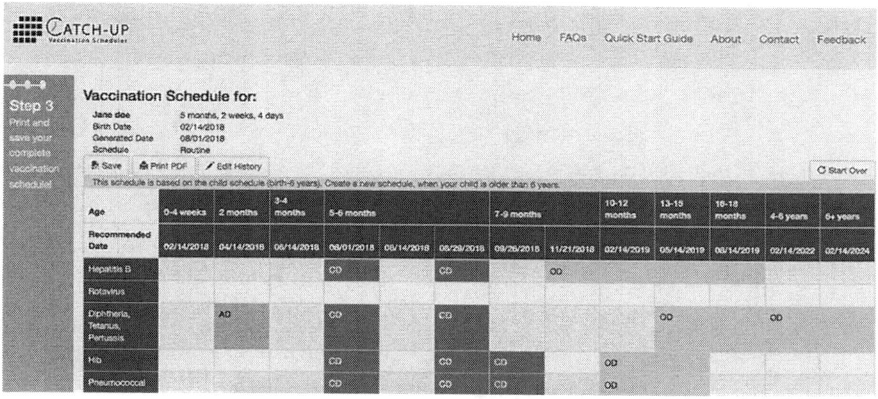

Figure 1.2. CDC Catch-Up Vaccination Scheduler Output

for their child, based on expert data regarding immunization schedules. Differently, for physicians, the application might represent a time-saving tool for generating vaccine schedules with patients. The Catch-Up Vaccination Scheduler takes the user through a series of steps. The first solicits a child's age and name.[25] Then the application returns a list of vaccines for the user to select as already administered vaccines.[26] Finally, a report is generated that includes a color-coded schedule for administering vaccines, including retroactive vaccine doses in red as "catch-up doses" or "CD" (figs. 1.1 and 1.2).[27]

Physicians who possess the wherewithal to "double-check" the outputs, might treat the web application as a tool for streamlining the decision-making process with patients. For patients, on the other hand, who might be less privy to current vaccine schedules and might not be programming savvy, the web application's actual calculations and database "under the hood" are mostly inaccessible, meaning that these users have to take the app at its word. And it is precisely because of this that the effect of the application, might invite an *ELIZA effect,* an effect that Noah Wardrip-Fruin describes as existing in those moments where users ascribe complexity to a system, based on front-end indicators of a given application, rather than understandings of what is actually happening on the back end. The effect is named after ELIZA, an early, famous chatbot that could engage communication in a seemingly open-ended manner, adapting to user input as a given conversation evolved over time. Drawing on an array of scholarly accounts of ELIZA from within human–computer interaction, Wardrip-Fruin explains that, despite being relatively simple in its programming, users who interacted with the bot nonetheless demonstrated a tendency to ascribe complexity to it. But, as Wardrip-Fruin elaborates, the ELIZA effect is subject to breakdown, based in the design parameters of the interface: "the illusion that something much more complex was going on inside the system (a human considering her problems seriously and answering questions thoughtfully, rather than random yes/no answers) [was able to be sustained] because the scope of possible responses was so limited. If it had been expanded only slightly—say, to random choice between the responses available in a 'magic eight ball'—almost any period of sustained interaction would have shattered the illusion through too many inappropriate responses."[28]

After one submits their data inputs to the Catch-Up Vaccination Scheduler, they are, for all intents and purposes "shaking the eight ball," interacting only with its outputs, seemingly inviting "more" than the impression of simplicity. Between the inputs of the user and the outputs of the system is the performance of the machine, carrying out its processes, in this case, vetting the ritual. The computational performance of the Catch-Up Vaccination Scheduler represents the energies of medical institutions and software engineers, wrought through the movements of a computing machine, carrying out calculations and referencing the most up-to-date data. "You will converse with an automated agent, who, of course, you associate with the deliberations of experts."

Clifford Nass and Youngme Moon offer the framework of *mindlessness* a for accounting for how, counterintuitively, humans tend to apply social scripts to computers, even when they are fully aware that the entity they are interacting with is a machine.[29] Saying "please" and "thank you," to a machine, moreover, is normal, based on mere routine and basal cues of interaction. Conversely, more

33 Manufactured Processing, Ritual, and Expert Systems

involved interactions that take forethought—like dealing with a complex emotion on the part of one's interlocutor—are less likely to invite mindless engagements of social script on the part of a human interacting with a computer. Important to Nass and Moon's contribution is their answer to *anthropomorphism* as a useful explanation for the phenomenon of applying social scripts to machines. Persons do not say "please" and "thank you" to a machine because they think it is human. Rather, people treat computers with polite interaction because they are not thinking about it—they are operating in rote, being mindless. Such rote scripts can be leveraged in ways that draw on deep genre ecologies, such as those characterized by knowledge-based systems and health science, carrying with them rituals that punctuate the energies of computing to offer a feeling to the user that the information being presented is reliable. Web applications, like the Catch-Up Scheduler, moreover, enliven communication at a nonconscious level, by speaking to human concerns with more-than-human energies.

After running from 2008 to 2020, the Catch-Up Scheduler was decommissioned.[30] In its place is the Child and Adolescent Vaccine Assessment Tool, a similar but simpler application still in use at the time of this writing (fig. 1.3).[31] Although its interface is similar to the Catch Up Scheduler, the newer Adolescent Vaccine Assessment Tool suggests vaccine names rather than output a vaccine schedule, alongside advice to consult one's doctor about obtaining those vaccines. In either case, the Catch-Up Scheduler and the Child and Adolescent Vaccine Assessment Tool both demonstrate examples in which the energies of computational performance can be leveraged to enliven legitimate health science. The recommendations of experts, in other words, are animated by the computational movements of these web applications, shaped by the rituals of interface interaction associated with the genre of public health knowledge-based systems as well as the longer standing trope of technologies of prophecy.

Although the apps referenced above are aligned with institutions of legitimate health science, one can enact the rituals traditionally associated with the league of scientific experts without actually requiring initiation as an expert. Experts in computer science and programming are not necessarily experts in anything beyond that. Even then, one does not have to be an expert in programming to cobble together existing libraries of code or to copy and paste others' computer coding projects, tweaking a few minor details to call it one's own. Despite this, one can use programming to create an automated agent that performs rituals of mainstream science, but without credentials to forward an argument to undermine mainstream science, beyond words, and beyond the

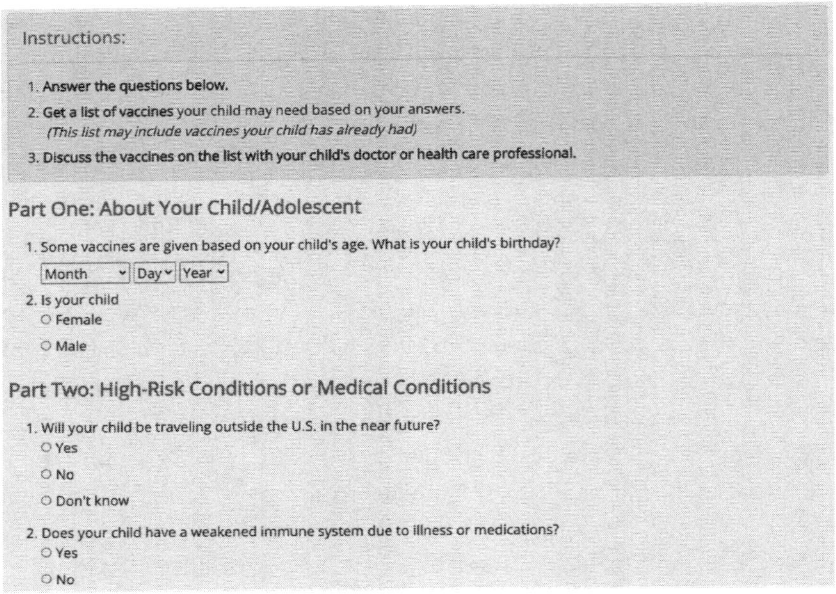

34 Influential Machines

Instructions:

1. Answer the questions below.
2. Get a list of vaccines your child may need based on your answers.
   (This list may include vaccines your child has already had)
3. Discuss the vaccines on the list with your child's doctor or health care professional.

Part One: About Your Child/Adolescent

1. Some vaccines are given based on your child's age. What is your child's birthday?
   [Month ▾] [Day ▾] [Year ▾]
2. Is your child
   ○ Female
   ○ Male

Part Two: High-Risk Conditions or Medical Conditions

1. Will your child be traveling outside the U.S. in the near future?
   ○ Yes
   ○ No
   ○ Don't know
2. Does your child have a weakened immune system due to illness or medications?
   ○ Yes
   ○ No

Figure 1.3. CDC Child and Adolescent Vaccine Assessment User Input Page

human. In doing so, the ritual of interacting with a knowledge-based system can be mimed within a computational performance, in turn cultivating a contented attunement to false medical advice based in pseudoscience.

What I hope to show in the following section, by untangling the social and technical scripts built into the pseudoscientific Vaccine Calculator, is that one can construct a mindless experience, which leverages the rhetorical energies of computational performance while emulating the ritualized procedures of interaction attendant to the tradition of knowledge-based systems, giving one's arguments a manufactured, but forceful, sense of legitimacy, spoken quietly through the movements of an automated agent, designed to feign a performance of legitimate health science.

The Manufactured Processing of Vaccine Calculator

Vaccine Calculator is a web application, designed by a volunteer at the National Vaccine Information Center, an organization dedicated to raising suspicion

35 Manufactured Processing, Ritual, and Expert Systems

of the safety of vaccines, framing it as "informed consent."[32] According to the application's homepage, Vaccine Calculator is "a simple tool to help make the calculations. . . . as a fundamental part of [peoples'] research to make the best decisions for themselves and their families."[33] It bears a striking resemblance to the CDC's Catch-Up Vaccination Scheduler.[34] But where the user experiences the Catch-Up Scheduler as an opportunity to more clearly understand the advice of experts, Vaccine Calculator emphasizes nonexpert understanding, an emphasis on patient-empowered "research." Where the CDC's Immunization Scheduler is built from the input of panels of medical science experts, Vaccine Calculator is the result of a single person who is aligned with the National Vaccine Information Center, a notoriously anti-vaccination leaning organization.[35] This person might possess expertise in web development but lacks credentials as an established expert in vaccine science. Nonetheless, according to the promotional copy written into the landing page of the application, Vaccine Calculator offers information for "hundreds of thousands of families from around the world" to use "as part of their informed vaccination decision-making research."[36]

Written in JavaScript, Vaccine Calculator generates outputs dynamically based on input data from the user, including "name," "age," "weight," and "allergies" to "egg" and "gelatin."[37] After the user has input their data and initiated an onclick event by clicking the submit button, a file loads containing thousands of lines of code. The main script for the application references a structured data set, which outlines specific vaccines and their corresponding values and then dynamically outputs ingredient data to the next page in correspondence to the data input by the user.[38] The script works from a data set, which (from looking at a file entitled "vic.csv" located on the "VaxCalc-Labs" public GitHub profile) seems to break out individual vaccines by "vaccine_type," "brand," "manufacturer," whether a vaccine has been "discontinued," the "name" of a given vaccine ingredient, "units," and units of measure, labeled as "uom."[39] Included in table 1.1 is an extract of the Hepatitis B vaccination entries. After the user clicks the submit button, they are brought to a second page and given a list of twenty-three checkboxes next to specific vaccines. Table 1.2 depicts this list.[40] Some of the vaccines in the list are accompanied by small .png image files, depicting an unborn fetus or a viral spore, meant to designate the presence of "human protein/DNA" or "live virus"—these are also indicated in the table.[41]

TABLE 1.1. Hepatitis B Excerpt from VaxCalc-Labs "Vaccine-Ingredients-Data"

VACCINE_TYPE	BRAND	MANUFACTURER	DISCONTINUED	NAME	UNITS	UNIT OF MEASUREMENT
HepB	Engerix-B (adult)	NULL	false	Aluminum	500.0	mcg
HepB	Engerix-B (pediatric)	NULL	false	Aluminum	250.0	mcg
HepB	Recombivax HB (adult)	NULL	false	Aluminum	500.0	mcg
HepB	Recombivax HB (adult)	NULL	false	Peptone, Soy	1.0	exposure
HepB	Recombivax HB (adult)	NULL	false	Formaldehyde	15.0	mcg
HepB	Recombivax HB (pediatric)	NULL	false	Aluminum	250.0	mcg
HepB	Recombivax HB (pediatric)	NULL	false	Formaldehyde	7.5	mcg

TABLE 1.2. List of Selections from "Step Two" of Vaccine Calculator

VACCINE	ACCOMPANYING IMAGE
DTaP: Diphtheria, Tetanus, Pertussis (ages 6 weeks through 6 years)	No Image
DTaP, Polio (Kinrix)	No Image
DTaP, HepB, Polio (Pediarix)	No Image
Hepatitis A	No Image
Hepatitis B	No Image
Hib: Haemophilus Influenza type b	No Image
HPV (Gardasil-9)	No Image
Influenza: Inactivated, egg-based	No Image
Influenza: Inactivated, without egg	No Image
Influenza: Intranasal	Viral Spore Image
MMR: Measles, Mumps, Rubella	Viral Spore Image Unborn Fetus Image
MMR, Chickenpox (ProQuad)	Viral Spore Image Unborn Fetus Image
Meningococcal ACWY (ages 11–18)	No Image
Meningococcal MPSV4 (age 55+)	No Image
Meningococcal B (age 10+)	No Image
PCV13: Pneumococcal conjugate (children 2 months–18 years)	No Image

38 Influential Machines

Table 1.2 continued

VACCINE	ACCOMPANYING IMAGE
PPSV23: Pneumococcal polysaccharide (adults 64 and older)	No Image
Polio	No Image
Rotavirus	Viral Spore Image
TDaP: Tetanus, Diphtheria, Pertussis (ages 7–64)	No Image
Td: Tetanus, Diphtheria	No Image
Varicella (Chickenpox)	Viral Spore Image Unborn Fetus Image
Herpes zoster (Shingles)	Viral Spore Image Unborn Fetus Image

When the user clicks the checkbox next to a given vaccine (e.g., the "Hepatitis B" vaccine), Vaccine Calculator generates a report toward the bottom of the page.[42] The report corresponds with the data input by the user. For a thirty-year-old person weighing one hundred pounds who selects the Hepatitis B vaccine, the application generates a bar graph, depicting "injected aluminum versus possibly safe for [name of user]," presented to the user in the form of red and green bars: "500mcg injected" vs. "180mcg possibly safe."[43] The very same input data with only the weight changed to two-hundred pounds and the same selection of the Hepatitis B vaccine gives this result: "500mcg injected" vs. "360mcg possibly safe."[44] Changing the age to 5 years old, 100 pounds, changes the output for the Hepatitis B vaccine to "250mcg injected" vs. "180mcg possibly safe." The results track along with the data set entries for the "pediatric" and "adult" Hepatitis B vaccine aluminum contents of the "vaccines-ingredients-data" (table 1.1). Based on testing, the pediatric results appear to stop at nineteen years old, and the adult results begin with entries of twenty years old.

After analyzing and testing the inputs and outputs of the system, I have found it is evident that the results are not very sophisticated. The only

39 Manufactured Processing, Ritual, and Expert Systems

meaningful shift in the information returned is in the difference between pediatric and adult doses. This information could easily be communicated by way of a table in a brochure or something of the sort; automation is not required to return these results. An answer to why someone might write a web application where one is not necessarily required is in the rhetorical energies of the computational performance. Enhancing the content of the table is the performance of an automated agent, "calculating" the results and returning them to the user in a manner that emulates the knowledge-based systems of legitimate health science. This is a pseudoscientific argument, given legitimacy by the movements of a machine.

Technically, Vaccine Calculator is not reporting false aluminum contents. According to the Engerix-B (Hepatitis B vaccine) insert, "Each .5-ML pediatric/ adolescent dose contains 10 mcg of HBsAg adsorbed on 0.25 mg [250 mcg] aluminum as aluminum hydroxide."[45] What is deceptive is the interpretation of that number. As the personalized Vaccine Calculator report states: "It is possibly safe for [user name] to receive 180 mcg per FDA recommended maximum daily aluminum dose of 4 to 5 mcg/kg/day to prevent accumulation and toxicity."[46] Anna Kata, in her study of the common argument points of vaccine denialists—and with regard to Vaccine Calculator specifically—explains that such an interpretation is misleading. Vaccine Calculator, by "comparing aluminum from a one-time vaccine dose to the daily estimated safe dose based on chronic, long-term exposure" is "making the vaccine dose appear dangerous."[47] Because Vaccine Calculator implies the movement of a machine in the background "running the numbers," the user is primed to believe that they are getting "facts" from which to draw their conclusions.

The process of inputting the data, clicking Submit, and awaiting a report on that data is a ritual associated with the practice and legitimacy of science. In this way, Vaccine Calculator invites the user to participate in the rituals of science, to manipulate outputs and to try different permutations, "including the ability to compare ingredients for the different brands of the same type of vaccine."[48] Being able to run different simulations and to be able to examine the outputs equips the user with just enough information to be able to feel competent enough to make a conclusion. In reality, the user is being given facts, reported out of context. Contrasted with the CDC's Catch-Up Scheduler, which was largely about relying on experts to "filter" out the clutter of possible data points so as to suggest a coherent plan of vaccination, Vaccine Calculator presents data to the user as a "wall" of information, affording the impression that the user is receiving "unfiltered" data, further exposing the general suspicion of expertise that undergirds the experience of the application. "I can figure this out on my own! I don't need your agenda!"

In light of Heidi Yoston Lawrence's insight that "fears of vaccination operate as more than just a set of discourses that express worry or conspiracy theories among the public but rather reflect *the unknown* as a material exigence," the leveraging of the rhetorical energies of knowledge-based systems in Vaccine Calculator can be seen as making an embodied appeal to an embodied concern.[49] Moreover, the concern is one of fear regarding the unknown threats of vaccination. As Brian Massumi articulates: "What is not actually real can be felt into being . . . fear is the anticipatory reality in the present of a threatening future. It is the felt reality of the nonexistent, looming present as the *affective fact* of the matter."[50] In the same way that a fire alarm can charge the body to be vigilant of the threat of a fire (even when there is no fire), Vaccine Calculator offers a "performative," or something that strikes the body as an indicator of threat.[51]

Put differently, the rhetorical effect of the Vaccine Calculator exists in its procedural reification of the existence of a threat (e.g., by repeatedly pointing to vaccines as dangerous), while augmenting with the energies of "calculation," inviting regard for the threat of vaccination as an affective fact. "If the data is returned, then the threat must exist!" Moreover, Vaccine Calculator represents a nonhuman performance, offering the appealing feeling of knowing, activated in the body by the movements of a computing machine, that is apparently just "running the numbers." This is especially so for those who might otherwise approach the risk / reward calculus of vaccination with a general sense of doubt.

Vaccine Calculator is a rhetorical construction that procedurally encourages the user to rationalize the threat of vaccination as real while augmenting with energies, punctuated by the prophetic rituals of expert systems to afford the feeling of staying "ahead of the threat." The Vaccine Calculator operates by cultivating an attunement that encourages a Dunning-Kruger effect in the user. The Dunning-Kruger effect is the phenomenon in which persons can overestimate their abilities within a given knowledge domain due to a lack of understanding in that domain.[52] Vaccine Calculator encourages users to feel false confidence regarding their understanding of vaccine safety by inviting them to "play the part" of the expert. By having an "expert system"—an automated agent—"report" the "data," the user can then apply their own self-knowledge, enacting their own agency as though they have competence in a particular

41 Manufactured Processing, Ritual, and Expert Systems

knowledge domain by endowing them with empty rituals of expertise, enlivened by computational movement.

Justin Kruger and David Dunning explain that some understanding of a given knowledge domain is necessary to allow for the overestimation of one's own competence. According to Kruger and Dunning, "in order for the incompetent to overestimate themselves, they must satisfy a minimal threshold of knowledge, theory, or experience that suggests to themselves that they can generate correct answers. In some domains, there are clear and unavoidable reality constraints that prohibits this notion. For example, most people have no trouble identifying their inability to translate Slovenian proverbs, reconstruct an 8-cylinder engine, or diagnose acute disseminated encephalomyelitis. In these domains, without even an intuition of how to respond, people do not overestimate their ability."[53]

Restated in terms of the energies of computational performance, the movements of the machine activate confidence, supported and punctuated by the rituals of knowledge-based systems and public health but ported to the expert-suspicious logics of vaccine denialist discourse. The user is invited to feel that they are adept at drawing conclusions regarding the safety of vaccination, when in fact they might not possess any actual competence in that knowledge domain. The ritual of Vaccine Calculator is not an authentic one; it is out of touch with scientific consensus regarding vaccine safety, risk, and benefit. Vaccine Calculator exploits instances of "meta-ignorance" about the topic of vaccination by supplanting with the movements of a machine to cultivate an attunement, a feeling of self-satisfaction in knowing that one is ahead of the threat of vaccination.[54] Built from scripts and databases and resonances with wider commitments to scientific suspicion, Vaccine Calculator performs as a machinic agent that inspires users to imagine themselves as experts, to identify with the rituals of legitimate health science.

Hillary A. Jones's discussion of identification in interactive, new media environments helps explain the process of identification that makes the Dunning-Kruger effect of Vaccine Calculator possible.[55] In particular, Jones argues that in online social media platforms like Pinterest, Instagram, Facebook, and Tinder, persons not only identify in the substance of the communications they share but in the practices of sharing—the energies of ritual. "Pinning, gazing, hashtagging, or swiping" are instances of human-computer interaction with which persons can identify.[56] Moreover, I can identify with my fellow "pinners" even if we are not pinning the same things to our boards. We share in identification, not because we share an "essential identity" but rather "shared forms and procedures"—we share in the ritual of "pinning."[57] The procedures of Vaccine Calculator are those that emulate other knowledge-based systems of public health and vaccine science by taking input data and returning a personalized report. By emulating these procedures, Vaccine Calculator enacts the rituals of legitimate public health and vaccine science, blurring the lines of difference between the rituals of legitimate science and a construction built to pantomime those rituals. Furthermore, by having the user engage the rituals of legitimate public health and vaccine science, they are being invited to identify with those realms of practice, equipping them with the (embodied) semblance of understanding needed to overestimate their competence to evaluate the scientific data that they are "analyzing"—to identify with experts of vaccine science, including "expert" machinic agents.

Moreover, because the interaction encouraged by Vaccine Calculator is one associated with the "muscle memory" of practices that can be associated with public health and vaccine science, the user is being primed to respond less cerebrally than if they were to locate the ingredients of a given vaccine, locate its tolerable aluminum content, and calculate the risk themselves. With respect to automated interface design, the interface of a knowledge-based system can call for "analytical cognition" on the part of the user, where connections and reasoning are necessary—the human needs to make sense of the computer outputs.[58] By contrast, an interface can also ask the user to respond with more "intuitive cognition" wherein the user responds more instinctually, based on recognition of patterns.[59] As demonstrated by other literatures on the "dual process" model of reasoning, analytic reasoning—also known as "System 2" reasoning—is activated in moments of "experienced difficulty" or "disfluency."[60]

Because Vaccine Calculator's performance is moored in the genre ecology of "expert" systems, an ecology that can be easily associated with legitimate public health and science, it can be said to include familiar cues that help the user feel "in the know," in turn encouraging System 1 reasoning at the instinctual end of the reasoning spectrum, making them comfortable with information they might not actually know anything about. Key to this effect are the rhetorical energies of the computational performance itself, in which the user is asked to participate with, and inadvertently identify with, the practices of experts (including expert automated agents), enlivened in the movements of the machine. Via manufactured processing, Vaccine Calculator is able to convince against scientific consensus, by way of appropriating the social and technical scripts—the rituals—one associates with the authority of scientific consensus and embedding them within a lively computational performance.

43 Manufactured Processing, Ritual, and Expert Systems

Put succinctly, Vaccine Calculator is a computational performance, characterized by the rhetorical tactic of manufactured processing, or the leveraging of the energies of computing machines to fabricate legitimacy for claims that are indefensible with respect to scientific consensus. In particular, Vaccine Calculator moves with the energy of an oracle to offer the "expert" advice to ignore the experts, beyond words, and beyond the human.

The Energetic Movements of "Experts" and Science Communication

Aimee K. Roundtree helps us further distinguish the difference between legitimate and manufactured processing in her examination of the rhetoric of computer simulations. In her thoughtful consideration of "virtual evidence," like visualizations of bumblebee flight and weather patterns, computer simulations manifest not as direct observations, but rather representations that nonetheless offer energy, an experience with the data "at work" (*energeia*)—the bringing of a phenomenon before the eyes, by way of looking across data points but not necessarily the phenomenon directly.[61] Such modeling is necessary in cases where the data points are so numerous or complex that they are difficult to perceive without first being modeled or filtered. The flights of small, industrious insects are difficult for the human eye to track in any meaningful way. And thus, Roundtree teaches us what is unique and powerful about computational media within the realm of science communication: it can bring knowledge and ideas "before the eyes," despite complexity. Conversely, as I hope that the current chapter has illuminated, the lively movements of computational performances—"running calculations"—can also be leveraged to enliven science communication—in some cases, illegitimately. Vaccine Calculator, moreover, enlivens pseudoscientific claims with the energies of machinic movements, animated by a deep end of computing permeated by rituals of knowledge-based systems as well as the longstanding trope of technologies of prophecy. Procedurally, Vaccine Calculator instantiates an argument, but vitalizing that argument are the movements of the machine between the front and back ends.

Because manufactured processing relies on the sorts of mindless associations between machines and science, it emerges as a troubling rhetoric of empowerment, wherein users are inspired to exercise their own agency. However, instead of being made comfortable with the conclusions of groups of experts, the user is made comfortable with conclusions that circulate within a problematic discourse ecology known to be suspicious of scientific consensus.

Such a happening can be juxtaposed against the phenomenon of citizen science, or the use of digital technologies to facilitate the participation of laypersons in the process of scientific inquiry (e.g., collecting data using sensors or participating in the analysis of data). Citizen science is sometimes conjectured to possess the potential to enhance publics' capacities for scientific thinking as well as their identification with scientists.[62] Rhetorically speaking, then (and as James Wynn points out), citizen science might be leveraged to counteract such phenomena as science denialism (although, as he would be careful to note, it is not a surefire strategy).[63] Vaccine Calculator invites laypersons to a similar experience—to feel like they are taking part of the rituals of science—when, in fact, they are doing pseudoscience. Consequently, the result can be said to be deleterious to people's capacities for scientific thinking, by leveraging a strategy that feels very similar to that of citizen science models of communication, but most emphatically lacks scientific credentials.

Manufactured processing is an alchemy of scientific legitimacy, which allows the user to equivocate the realms of self-knowledge with scientific knowledge. In this way, manufactured processing is not merely a reification of the idea that procedures can be used persuasively. Rather, manufactured processing teaches us that the energies of computing, at least insofar as they are associated with the rituals of interaction associated with self-moving machines endemic to particular knowledge domains, can be appropriated to add scientific legitimacy to claims that are in actuality pseudoscientific. It is when we put concepts of computing in conversation with rhetorical practice that we realize that, beyond the front ends (interfaces) and the back ends (databases) of computing systems, there is also a (mindless) deep end of computing, where the rituals of oracles and prophets interact with the genre ecologies of knowledge-based systems, animating some computational performances, such as Vaccine Calculator.[64]

This chapter pursued the epistemic end in an interactive computational performance. In the next chapter I examine the aesthetic end of rhetorical energy in a computational performance that does not involve user interaction per se, but nonetheless imbues sublime energies through the processual magnitude of vast computing.

2

Processual Magnitude, the Sublime, and Computational Poiesis

Christ of the Abyss is a bronze figure of Christ, submerged fifteen meters beneath the surface of the Mediterranean Sea, near San Fruttuoso, Italy.[1] It was cast and placed in 1954 by Guido Galletti, in honor of Dario Gonzatti, a famous Italian diver. The statue, by many accounts, is a beautiful sight. It sits on the ocean floor, raising its hands to the glass ceiling of the ocean. Refracted sunlight spills down onto the visage of Christ. In this particular piece, beyond the brilliance of the artist, one might also find themselves in awe of the scratches and chips in the surface of the statue, the sea crustaceans living in its pitted metal—the natural processes that have become entangled with it. While the statue can be said to be beautiful, one could also make the argument that the statue is sublime, invoking a simultaneous experience of awe and fear in the face of the relentless, uncontrollable energies of nature. One could argue further that the impact of this piece of art exists somewhere between the hand of Galletti and the flows of currents, life cycles of crustaceans, and erosive qualities of bronze. The human energies of the statue are entangled with nonhuman ones, affording vastness—magnitude—to the experience of Christ of the Abyss, which, in turn, does not offer a sense of cohesion, or closedness to the experience, but rather an unresolvedness, an open-endedness, experienced beyond words, and born from beyond the human, marking a unique experience, enlivened by nonhuman energies as they interact with human ones.

In this chapter, I wish to pursue a similar experience of sublime magnitude within a case of computational performance: a Twitterbot called @censusAmericans. @censusAmericans sources census data to tell pithy stories about real US citizens and will continue to do so on the hour, every hour, for the next millennium. The liveliness of the bot, despite appearing more artificial, implies a magnitude on the scale of natural processes, representing

46 Influential Machines

energies similar to Christ of the Abyss in that they are set in motion by human hands, but involve unpredictable emergence beyond them. As such, the bot represents a unique rhetorical tactic located precisely in its lively computational movement beyond human control and comprehension, or what I will call *processual magnitude*: the use of vast computational performance to afford not a sense of coherence, but of irresolution. Building from the notion of the computational sublime, this chapter will show that animating the front and back ends of the performance of @censusAmericans, from within the deep end of computing, are category assumptions regarding "natural" and "artificial," categories that are disrupted when they are activated simultaneously by the bot's lively (but not alive) movements, the result of which is an invitation toward an X-ray sublime experience—a sustained sense of irresolution, activated by the performance of infinity "at work."

Amid discourse ecologies, marred by such phenomena as "filter bubbles" and "political polarization," wherein publics have difficulty in considering subject positions beyond their own, vast computational performance (counterintuitive as it may be) springs forth as a means by which to cultivate attunements that facilitate further questioning of one's own being-in-the-world.[2] Such is a prospect for appreciating what it is that computational performance can do for public life. To unpack the sublime performance of @censusAmericans, I first discuss the rhetorical aesthetics of magnitude, while tracking a useful distinction between the beautiful and the sublime.

The Aesthetics of Vast Computing

As a rhetorical tactic, magnitude is often discussed with regard to the piling of diction or the use of grand metaphors, or even the practice of creating and visualizing immense archives of information—verbal and visual discourses, created and spoken by humans to cultivate a sense of conviction.[3] For example, Jenny Rice builds from the work of Aristotle and explains that the aesthetic experience of magnitude (*megethos*) can be facilitated by networked, digital media technologies to become *archival magnitude:* "an aesthetic inflection of a quantitative mass that gives a sense of weightiness, a sense that sustains the epistemic without relying on epistemology to structure it."[4] Magnitude, performed in the construction and citation of large databases of "evidence" by science denialists, for instance, offers a feeling of resolution to their claims, by seemingly locating it in the transcendence of individual perspective while emulating networked rituals of science communication.[5] "Look, we have a database. We'll visualize

47 Processual Magnitude, the Sublime, and Computational Poiesis

the data. HIV doesn't cause AIDS." Important to this, for Rice, is that the performance of archival magnitude, say in the aesthetics of big data visualizations, is "a *sense* of something coherent, a sense that possibly transcends the individual pieces of datum that are contained within that aesthetic whole."[6] The performance of archival magnitude is a means of amassing human rhetorical energies in support of one's claims (regardless of factual basis), seemingly to foreclose reproach—to negate the drive to ask more questions. Magnitude can also be used in new media contexts to add coherence in the face of oppressive social structures that might support unmerited questions, as Stephanie Larson demonstrates in her compelling analysis of the #MeToo hashtag, in which she analyzes the hashtag as a vast list of stories, representing the magnitude of the problem of sexual violence, by accumulating sensations of pain to garner attention and motivate audiences to action in the face of patriarchy.[7] In either archival magnitude or the magnitude of vast lists, magnitude can be characterized as *coherentizing,* or "beautiful" (in the technical sense of the word), which Immanuel Kant, in his *Critique of the Power of Judgement,* defines as an aesthetic construction, which represents harmony and symmetry, fixed in a bounded object (such as a data visualization or a hashtag).[8] And as Rice and Larson have compellingly demonstrated, phenomena like archival magnitude or the magnitude of vast lists are beautiful ones, which leverage immense amounts of human energy to afford feelings of coherence to a public, either to foreclose reproach or to maintain resilience, despite unwarranted reproach.

By contrast, there exists another aesthetic, manifest as magnitude, but which can emerge from beyond the human: the sublime. Sublime experiences are moored in difficult-to-comprehend quantities and forces, which are characterized by a complex mixture of enjoyment and horror found in the pleasurable experience of an object that transcends human control and comprehension as a boundless object worthy of respect.[9] (Thunderstorms are often used as an example of the sublime.) In contrast to beautiful magnitude, sublime magnitude, rather than encouraging a sense of coherence, cultivates a sense of disarray, located in the overwhelming of the imagination's ability to comprehend. With concern for magnitude as an overwhelming experience in the context of machine communication, sublime magnitude is distinct from something like Jonathan Bradshaw's rhetorical exhaustion. In cases of rhetorical exhaustion, technologies, like bots, can be used to repeat and amplify one's claims in ways that overwhelm publics, offering not a sense of coherence, but rather a sense of exhaustion, sapping energy through amplification, reducing motivation to engage.[10]

48 Influential Machines

Computational performances characterized by sublime magnitudes of computing, on the other hand, even if they are attended by angsty attunements (more on this later), overwhelm with their unpredictable, uncontrollable energies, nonetheless motivating further questioning: "What is my story? What is theirs? What matters in a story?" The immense storytelling of @censusAmericans makes clear that the processual magnitude of some computational performances represent sublime energies, which can be leveraged strategically to influence publics by invoking a sense of irresolution, located not just in the widgets produced by their operations ("Look at this procedurally generated story!"), but also in their (un)natural scale of movement ("Whoa! This bot will continue to tweet poems for the next millennium!").

The sublime blurring of the "natural" and the "artificial" in technological discourses is not necessarily new territory for rhetorical scholarship. But within this territory, the sublime is often invoked with concern for utopian myths perpetuated in discourse about technology, rather than artistic performances and experiences entangled with lively movements of technology. For example, In their description of the rhetoric of the electrical sublime, James W. Carey and John J. Quirk point to an underlying myth of "electrical utopia," a technologically deterministic discourse, guiding policy and relations. Electrical utopia "invests electricity with the capacity to produce automatically, on the one hand, power, productivity and prosperity and, on the other, peace, a new and satisfying form of human community and a harmonious accord with nature."[11] Such is an approach to a problematic discourse, facilitated by an aesthetic of technology as a natural force. In Carey and Quirk's words: "The first task is to demythologize the rhetoric of the electronic sublime. Electronics is neither the arrival of apocalypse nor the dispensation of grace. Technology is technology; it is a means for communication and transportation over space, and nothing more."[12]

Similarly, David Nye has noted that the sublime in technology can be accompanied by appeals moored in the rational domination of nature (e.g., the technological sublime) or the movement of forward progress (e.g., the electrical sublime).[13] Similarly, Vincent Mosco tracks the utopian promise of "cyberspace" to transcend physical geography and to flatten political hierarchy, as it is entangled with corporate discourse.[14] Nye's and Mosco's ideas have been considered in the context of algorithms by Morgan Ames. In Ames's view, algorithms are accompanied by the myth of algorithms as impenetrable "black boxes."[15] Consequently, the goal in studying algorithms and their entanglements with culture is to "dispel the *algorithmic sublime* that characterizes contemporary

49 Processual Magnitude, the Sublime, and Computational Poiesis

discourses on algorithms" by cracking open the black box—to learn about how particular algorithms operate—to counter the myth by showing how algorithmic processes are shaped by, and shape, cultural practices of surveillance, for instance.[16] These approaches to the sublime and technological discourse are enlightening with regard to how we conceive of, and talk about, technology, enhancing critical sensibilities by offering tools for parsing (and illustrating the blurring of) the mythic, the natural, the technical, and the cultural. And, as such, the dispelling of the myth of the sublime in technological contexts is useful for critical thinking. By the same token, however, such approaches largely interrogate the sublime in the pejorative, leaving by the wayside the potential artistic merits of sublime experiences, such as that offered by the performance of a Twitterbot, which will ceaselessly tweet stories—exert energies—without rest or repose, for the next millennium.

To demonstrate the leveraging of the sublime energies of computational performance, I now move to an analysis of both the front and the back ends of @censusAmericans, a Twitter bot that is splendidly simple in its programming but represents vastness in the energies of its computational performance.

The Sublime Energies of @censusAmericans

@censusAmericans is a Twitterbot that earned some buzz within the botmaker community, and in the broader artistic community, where, for instance, its impacts can be found as resonating into the work of other artists who wrote music to accompany the bot.[17] The bot runs on Twitter, sourcing US census data to generate and tweet small biographical statements about individual, anonymous persons. For example: "I work in machine shops; turned products; screws, nuts and bolts. I don't have health insurance. I have been married twice. I am divorced."[18] The creator, Jia Zhang, crafted the bot as a graduate student who was affiliated with the Massachusetts Institute of Technology Social Computing Group. As she writes in a *FiveThirtyEight* article, which details the project: "CensusAmericans will insert strangers into your life at regular intervals and will continue its automated task until it gets to the end of the 15,450,265 rows in the data set. That'll only take about 1,760 years."[19] Such is an instance of computational performance that confronts persons with processes beyond control and prediction; it is a sublime experience.

Artists / scholars Jon McCormack and Alan Dorin have developed an account of the aesthetic experience enmeshed with generative computational art (i.e., art made via random or mutative processes in a program). Specifically, they develop an account of the *computational sublime:* "the instilling of simultaneous feelings of pleasure and fear in the viewer of a process realized in a computing machine, a duality in that even though we cannot comprehend the process directly, we can experience it through the machine—hence we are forced to relinquish control. It is possible to realize processes of this kind in the computer due to the speed and scale of its internal mechanism, and because its operations occur at a rate and in a space vastly different to the realm of our direct perceptual experience."[20]

Integral to McCormack and Dorin's computational sublime is the concept of *emergence,* that which manifests beyond human control and prediction—poiesis, born of the human hand, but "at work" beyond it, and thus, in turn, taking on a character of natural processes: "It offers both pleasure and fear: pleasure in the sense that here inside a finite space is the representation (and partial experience) of something infinite to be explored at will; fear in that the work is in fact infinite, and also in that we have lost control."[21] The energies of some computational performances, despite being artificial, move in ways that feel natural, as in emerging beyond human control. Within this framing, the performance of a Twitter bot can be aesthetically powerful, not just because of what it says, but also how it moves; its lively energies strike the body in ways (un)natural.

Every hour a new micro-story about a United States citizen is shared by @censusAmericans, representing an ongoing, unresolved performance: "Last time I got married was in 1996. I have been married twice. I am divorced. I work in medical equipment and supplies. I drive to work."[22] The richness of the bot's stories, including its blemishes, grows over time, amassing the outputs of its work on the front end: "I work from home. I don't have health insurance. I work in miscellaneous retail stores. I have multiple ancestries."[23] One could copy one of these tweets from @censusAmericans and share it elsewhere; one might even print out all of the tweets to date and publish them in a book. However, those copies would be missing the experience of visiting the site of the bot directly. Intimately woven into this is the exhilaration of seeing the newest tweet to pop up in the feed; the result of an automated system working on the back end, randomly parsing data and tweeting within the parameters of a Python script—the "other half" of the movements of the machine as it performs its art-making. @censusAmericans, as it exists at its Twitter account, is characterized by a lively computational performance, something which is only decayed when copied away from its site online, where the bot performs the work of art.

51 Processual Magnitude, the Sublime, and Computational Poiesis

From looking at Zhang's GitHub profile, where she has made her source code public, it can be seen that the bot is composed of three different scripts, written in the programming language Python.[24] The first script, "draft.py," sources and structures raw data from the United States Census Bureau's "2013 Public Use Microdata."[25] The second script, "refine.py," takes that structured data and randomly generates three or four sentences, sourcing individual categories from the census data form, while checking that they fit within a 140-character limit.[26] The third script, "censusAmericansBot.py," posts the final set of sentences to Twitter.

According to the "Read Me" file accompanying the code, Zhang wrote the third script while working from the basis of "everywordbot," a Twitter bot written by Allison Parrish, an instructor in the Interactive Telecommunications Program at New York University. Also important to note is that the code located in the Python script posted to Zhang's public GitHub repository indicates a "time.sleep(14400)," which means that each tweet should happen every four hours, after a 14400-second "sleep." As it exists on Twitter, however, it is evident that @censusAmericans is posting every hour. There is also some evidence that the version of the code on the GitHub account is set to make "tweets," 3–4 sentences long, whereas the bot "in the wild" shows evidence of at least 5. As such, the analysis will attempt to triangulate between both the source code accessible on GitHub and the output on the Twitter profile itself in accounting for the energies of its computational performance.[27]

Surely Zhang's artistic hand is present in the coding. In fact, some would be quick to recognize the "craftiness" of her ability to hack census data and work within the constraints of Python as a programming language to create art.[28] In addition to appreciating Zhang's artistry, however, the viewer also comes to the site to see what the bot will do. Each tweet is the result of computational processes. For example, the script "draft.py" makes it possible for "column JWTR with value 06" to be "translated into 'I take a ferryboat to work'."[29] Then, after that script runs, it is passed off to "refine.py," which tries multiple permutations of the conversational sentences generated from "draft.py" until a tweet is crafted containing at least three sentences, but not more than four, falling within a 140-character restriction.[30] Finally, "censusAmericansBot.py" sources each set of sentences and, using the Twitter application programming interface, it then posts that set as a unique message to the Twitter account, @censusAmericans, once every hour.[31] For example: "I work in electric lighting and electrical equipment manufacturing. I got married in 1969. I have a high

52 Influential Machines

school diploma. I am married."[32] The scripts undergirding @censusAmericans, "draft.py" and "censusAmericansBot.py" are the least exciting scripts; they are simply populating a data object with the values of the census data or automatically posting results to Twitter. However, there is vital randomness involved in the third script, "refine.py," which demonstrates the sublimity of the bot's lively movements.

With "refine.py," Zhang is essentially handing off the census data to the system to compose a tweet, sourcing the original sentences culled from the census data file, ultimately, to decide what will make it into the final tweet and in what order. Note the random.sample() method employed in the following excerpt of the script, highlighted in bold. Note also the bits of code that follow "#"s, as these are essentially working scripts, likely leftover from originally testing the operation of the bot, which would be helpful to the coder for tracking specific portions of the processes of the bot (i.e., to print to screen the values of a working variable).

```
while len(newRowText) > 140 and rowLength > 3:
        sampling = random.sample(range(1, len(newRow)), rowLength- 1)
        rowLength = rowLength-1
        #print sampling
        shorttweet = ""
        for i in sampling:
                shorttweet += str(newRow[i])
        #print len(shorttweet)
#print newLine
        #print shorttweet
if shorttweet in existingtweets:
        print "repeat"
else:
        spamwriter.writerow([shorttweet])
```
[33]

What random.sample() is doing in this script is referencing a list of sentences previously generated by "draft.py" and choosing 3–4 of them. For a simple example, if one has a list of four items that is defined as cutesyExampleList = ["kitten," "puppy," "bear," "squirrel"] and they apply random.sample() while defining that they only want two items from the list, it could be expressed as random.sample(cutesyExampleList, 2), which would produce something like ["squirrel," "kitten"]. Important here is that random.sample() does not

53 Processual Magnitude, the Sublime, and Computational Poiesis

just grab random items, it also randomizes the ordering of the output. In this sense, Zhang has designed the system to engage in the four basic rhetorical operations: omission, addition, transposition, and transmutation, defined in *Rhetorica Ad Herennium*.[34] The machine is omitting, adding, transposing, and transmuting content. The initial script, "draft.py" transmutes census data into sentences, and "refine.py" adds, omits, and transposes those sentences into individual tweets. While Zhang is the writer of the bot, the bot is the lively entity performing the work of writing the tweets, enacting rhetorical action, characterized by a vastness, beyond words. As such, @censusAmericans invites the witness to simultaneously feel gratification and anxiety amid the open-ended, unanswerable character of infinity "at work," implied by a computational performance wherein control has been surrendered to the generative activities of the machine, beyond prediction. Existing in @censusAmericans are Zhang's energies in writing Python scripts. But alongside Zhang's energies are those of the machine, carrying out its scripts to create on its own, invoking awe, born of the smashing *physis* (the chaos of nature) into *poiesis* (the organization of nature for human purpose).

Just as we might appreciate a painter's ability to work from primary pigments to create signature tones and work with brushes to create an image of a human face—to work within "constraints"—so too can one appreciate Zhang's brilliance of programming. Notable here is that artists and constraints are different. Artists work within constraints to turn things into art; conversely, the automated system that undergirds @censusAmericans is not merely a constraint on creation, but rather an entity also working under constraints set by Zhang. Integral to the energies one can experience at the site of @censensusAmericans is the difficulty in distinguishing which choices belong to Zhang, and which ones belong to the automated system. "Is the program a constraint on Zhang, or the other way around?" The notion that the creation of the bot exists between the nonhuman and the human, where, apparently, art "just happens" offers an experience, characterized by energies that enigmatize distinctions between the artificial and the natural, but manifest as machinic movement.

Crucially, the performance of infinity and the loss of control that characterize the performance of @censusAmericans is a unique melding of two types of sublime experience. Drawing on a Kantian framework of the sublime, McCormack and Dorin explain that some computational art can demonstrate both the *mathematical sublime* (the idea of infinity) as well as the *dynamical sublime* (the distanced experience of threat). The mathematical sublime designates experiences in which the limits of one's ability to comprehend an idea are surpassed, exposing to a person the limits of their own capacity, leaving them to feel inadequate, but in a manner that springs forth an enjoyable moment for having the thought in the first place.[35] The immensity of St. Peter's Basilica, for example, can leave the viewer with "a feeling of the inadequacy of . . . [their] imagination for presenting the ideas of a whole, in which the imagination reaches its maximum and, in the effort to extend it, sinks back into itself, but is thereby transported into an emotionally moving satisfaction."[36] The dynamical sublime, on the other hand, exists in moments where one is confronted with an uncontrollable threat, but experienced at a distance, leaving the viewer to ponder limits of their own power, but while also offering an enjoyable consideration of one's own strength beyond the usual limits.[37] A violent thunderstorm off in the distance or the eruption of a volcano instantiate experiences that "allow us to discover within ourselves a capacity for resistance . . . which gives us the courage to measure ourselves against the apparent all-powerfulness of nature."[38] In McCormack and Dorin's frame, computational artworks can include both categories in that they can imply infinity beyond human comprehension (the mathematical sublime) as well as loss of control to the processes of the machine (the dynamical sublime). In both cases, however (and important to the current discussion of rhetorical energy, which is concerned with the moods/attunements that attend computational performances), there is a need to adapt McCormack and Dorin's Kantian framework of the sublime slightly.

That is, Kant's sublime is an experience that involves emotion, but which is actualized in cerebral exercise, finding resolution in rational reflection—thoughts, rather than moods. The sublime, in Kant's view, "is the disposition of the mind resulting from a certain representation occupying the reflective judgment," for "that is sublime which even to be able to think of demonstrates a faculty of the mind that surpasses every measure of the senses."[39] Consequently, Kant's sublime, even if it originates from an emotional experience, finds resolution in rational thought more than feeling. As it concerns an investigation of the rhetorical energies of vast computational performance, which is expressly concerned with the attunements of the body, Kant's sublime is left wanting as it seems to locate rational thought, rather than embodied attunement, as the linchpin of sublime experience. This is a limitation in that computational performance can capitalize on vastness not to offer a cerebral resolution, but rather a sustained, ambient feeling of irresolution as can be seen in @censusAmericans' lively movements.

55 Processual Magnitude, the Sublime, and Computational Poiesis

To better account for such irresolution born of magnitude, I expound upon the Kantian notion of the sublime by drawing on Carolyn Kane's X-ray sublime and connecting it to computational performance. Kane, building on the work of Giles Deleuze, explains her X-ray sublime as an inversion of the longstanding Kantian view of the sublime as an "unhinged state of mind in the subject, triggered by worldly representations that occupy the energies of both the imagination and reflective judgment, but are ultimately appeased by the latter."[40] The X-ray sublime is an experience of the sublime, characterized not by rational resolution, but rather the feeling of unresolvedness—the lack of closure, continual open-endedness. (The removal of the "taking" of imagination by reason also is a clever way to approach the sublime in a manner that carefully moves forward from an aesthetic tradition marred by problematic gender binaries such as reason as masculine or beauty as feminine, for instance.)[41]

As Kane elaborates, "the failure to provide resolution is also at the heart of my concept of the X-ray sublime, which turns on the inversion of classical and modern aesthetic pursuits for unification and cohesive symbolization. The X-ray sublime does not overcome itself but instead lands in constant and perpetual chaos."[42] As an example of the X-ray sublime, Kane gives an aesthetic reading of Edward Burtynsky's e-waste photographs, which depict the horrible working and living conditions wrought by e-waste disposal around the globe, foregrounding intricate messes of color and figure in the form of wires or discarded electronics parts. According to Kane, the images create a tension between pleasure and fear, posing a question, rather than an answer, productively invoking a state of openness to reconsider one's place in, and effect on, the world. The "impossibility" of Burtynsky's photographs "implicates *us,* not just 'them'," withholding closure, asking the viewer: "Can you look at this peacefully, undisturbed? And even if the answer is yes, then the image has at least done the work of raising the question."[43]

For all of the promise Kane finds in the sublime for helping persons move toward better relations, she is doubtful of the mathematical sublime, for the experience, which is moored in the grandness of ideas—like infinity—beyond the human capacity to grasp them, "is further removed and abstracted, not only from landscape, but also from concrete experience."[44] It is easy to agree with Kane, for it seems that invoking unresolved tensions tracks better with the dynamical sublime—powerful forces, beyond human control, threatening imposition into one's sphere of living—because it affords embodied considerations of one's own, and others', lifeworlds, to feel differently, rather than just think differently. But within the frame of rhetoric as energy, and within the context of the computational performance of @censusAmericans, it is evident that, by way of the lively movements of the performance, even the mathematical sublime—the idea of infinity—is rendered through the movements of the machine; it is transduced into the body, and in a way that cultivates an attunement to those borders between human and nonhuman, artificial and natural, instantiating an embodied experience with the uncanny.

Distinct from still images, or elevated language, computational performances are multimodal in their liveliness, and by consequence, as Minsoo Kang explains in his *Sublime Dreams of Living Machines,* their movements (especially movements that mimic animal and human behavior) pushes one toward an uncanny sublimity, which "pos[es] an ever greater danger to our reality schema based on the categories of the animate/inanimate, natural/artificial, and living/dead," while at the same time, "it is indeed only a machine, no matter how good it is at pretending to be a living being."[45] Consequently, dynamical sublimity of computational performances is spawned from a loss of control (as McCormack and Dorin maintain), but also in flashes of existential threat to humanity's understanding of itself, wherein the imagination reaches its own limits of understanding (as Kang posits). "What is this? What am I?" As such, @censusAmericans animates an X-ray sublime experience, realized in the existential threat of an entity, which can move beyond the scope of human control and comprehension, imposing energies that strike the viewer as threatening precisely because they represent an unbounded magnitude, moored in creation beyond prediction—the idea of infinity "at work."

Consequently, the sublimity of @censusAmericans is uncanny, performing more-than-human energies, entangled with human ones. For example, @censusAmericans will continue to generate micronarratives for 1760 years (an unfathomable length of time in contrast to the human lifetime). Knowing that this is something that could continue well after one's own lifetime brings the realization that the bot will create things that, as of yet, are waiting to emerge, but which are also incomprehensible. This can be just as exciting as it can be disconcerting, for the bot is confronting human viewers with their own mortality—their own insignificance—contrasted to the magnitude of the cosmos. Bewildering and astonishing, @censusAmericans invites the viewer to experience vastness, open-endedness, unpredictability—things that characterize the awe of natural processes—but distinctly as the consequence of (non)human *poiesis.* Put differently, each new biographical tweet generated by the steadfast computational processes that undergird @censusAmericans

57 Processual Magnitude, the Sublime, and Computational Poiesis

encourages questions rather than answers: "Who is this person?" "To what life projects do they belong?" "How do my projects relate?" And enlivening these questions are the sublime energies of the machine, operating with the vastness of nature, imposing simultaneously a dynamical sublimity, located in the existential threat posed by a nonliving, but lively, entity and a mathematical sublimity, located in the movements of the machine as it performs infinity "at work."

In summary, @censusAmericans offers an illustration of the uniquely influential energies of vast computational performance, which can be leveraged rhetorically to offer not a sense of cohesion—a reification of belief—but a sustained sense of unresolvedness, an X-ray sublime experience, not just in dynamical terms (i.e., immense force), but also in mathematical terms (i.e., infinity "at work"). What @censusAmericans teaches us is that the loss of control and existential threat of machinic movement in some computational performances can vitalize not a sense of coherence, but rather a sense of irresolution.

Attuning to the Angst of @censusAmericans

Internet artist and fellow bot-maker Darius Kazemi praises Zhang's @census Americans as delivering "devastating summaries of the lives of real Americans culled from census data. It is poetry. Jia Zhang is brilliant."[46] With concern to the transformation of data into art, it is more than easy to agree with Kazemi. Zhang's bot takes "found" things that exist in something as humdrum and monotonous as census data and transforms them into pithy opportunities for viewers to ask the question that Kane articulates in her explanation of the X-ray sublime: "Can I look at this peacefully undisturbed?"[47] But beyond being a brilliant piece of art, @censusAmericans also represents a unique tactic that can be leveraged influentially and that is moored specifically in the movements of a lively, but not alive, performance of computing.

Debra Hawhee helps us understand the uniqueness of the aesthetics of @censusAmericans through her reading of *On the Sublime,* and specifically, in (Pseudo-)Longinus's commentary on the divine horses of Homer's *Illiad,* wherein, the "cosmic strides [of the divine horses] are awe-inspiring precisely because they bear reference to—and radically outpace—the comprehensible, earth-bound strides of human-guided horses."[48] Homer, a human, wrote the story, but the power of the magnitude is facilitated by the energies of the nonhuman. Important here is that the nonhuman does not make the sublime per se, but rather it is the energy of the nonhuman operating beyond one's sphere of influence and understanding, which Longinus would elaborate does "not . . . persuade the audience but rather . . . transport[s] them out of themselves."[49] Similarly, Zhang wrote @censusAmericans, but the bot nonetheless moves on its own, representing energies in its stories, located precisely in the fact that they are written beyond human control. Rather than tapping into the energies of the machine metaphorically through language, it performs infinity "at work," energies at magnitudes that dwarf human comprehension and ability, to transport one "out of themselves."

Because it confronts the witness with a displacement of self-understanding, @censusAmericans can be described as cultivating an attunement to angst, a ground-mood, ever-present, concealed under the stability of one's everyday lifeworld.[50] As Matthew Ratcliffe explains, the phenomenological experience of angst implies a momentary but "radical transformation of the ordinarily taken-for-granted sense of belonging to a world, where the usual sense of things as practically significant is gone from experience."[51] With the experience of angst, even if only for a moment, comes "the sense that anything *is* significant, ever *was* significant or ever *could be* significant is absent."[52] Preconceptions of value and commitment are suspended. Plans for the future are forgotten. Dwelling on the past is traded for open attunement to new possibilities of possibility. With this shift in attunement comes increased openness, a receptivity to ideas and feelings perhaps closed off by the previously concealed mores of one's own lifeworld. Where some might argue that angst is something to be considered as an undesirable state, wherein rhetoric can be employed to make noisy archives more "tolerable" by offering structure, @censusAmericans demonstrates that perhaps angsty attunements can also be desirable, exposing that the sublime energies of vast computing can cultivate openness, rather than closedness, in association with the biographical data of real people and their own situations in the world.[53]

In the psychological literatures, "perspective-taking," or "actively imagining how the other is affected by [their] plight," is considered an antecedent to "empathic concern," which is a state associated with behaviors like helping others in need.[54] In these literatures, the ability to appreciate and understand others is often conceived as a "work in progress," requiring practice, including hypothetical, imaginative practice. Psychologists Michael W. Myers and Sara D. Hodges explain further that, "as interactions unfold over time, mental constructions such as schemas and simulations may become increasingly more

59 Processual Magnitude, the Sublime, and Computational Poiesis

important sources of information for the perceiver than the actual behavior of the target person during the interaction."[55] That is, the more scenarios one can imagine themselves into, the better equipped they will be to attune to the other when confronted with an actual interaction with another person. Important to note is that the effect of @censusAmericans is similar to the ambient music that Rickert analyzes in his *Ambient Rhetoric:* it "organizes an experience, not so much to persuade in any direct sense, but to attune and inflect our sense of bodily inhabitance and the cradle of intelligibility within which we comport ourselves."[56] In the case of @censusAmericans, perspective-taking is enlivened not simply by the energies of other humans, but the more-than-human energies imbued by the "natural" movements of a lively (but not alive) entity, which implies infinity "at work," encouraging an attunement to angst, a permeating of lifeworld, opening newly embodied considerations of the lifeworlds of others: "I walk to work. I get to work around 1:15pm. I am looking for work. I work for the state government. I don't have health insurance."

While one could argue that the ambiguity of the individual stories told by @censusAmericans makes it possible for a person to easily put themselves in the other's "shoes," it is more profound to notice that the machinic energies of the bot's performance invoke a uniquely sublime magnitude, affecting the viewer with a sustained sense of unresolvedness and further implicating an attunement of angst. Consequently, processual magnitude is not just something to behold as a novelty of machine-generated art; it is something that can be strategically employed in contexts that demand expansions of lifeworld, broaches toward empathy.

Doing More with Computational Performance

The positive implications of the sublime energies of vast performance are not positioned here as a retort to scholars who remain skeptical of communication technology or those who might find automation itself to be entangled with dangerous ideologies, hidden under appeals to progress.[57] Nor is the analysis a naive perpetuation of technological utopianism. Rather, the analysis should be read for what it is: an effort to understand the rhetorical implications of vast computational performance. As a case, @censusAmericans demonstrates that the energies of computational performance can be leveraged through processual magnitude affording an X-ray sublime experience, located in the simultaneous activation of the "artificial" and the "natural" by an entity that moves as infinity "at work," enlivening the imagination, not with a sense of coherence, but a sense of unresolvedness. Jia Zhang's computational art, moreover, is positive, deep, and moving, not simply because of the stories it tells, but also the lively way it moves.

Kevin Brock has made an extended argument for the importance of analyzing computationally driven texts with specific regard for the back-end processes that undergird them, for those processes, in a manner unique to computational media, shape experience in ways distinct from strictly verbal texts, moored in time-based performance and often the processes themselves.[58] The current chapter extends Brock's insights to show that when connections are made between the front and back ends of computational performances, one can expose the sorts of confusing, complex, and incoherent habits of being that can be activated by the energies of computing. The case study of this chapter illustrates those habits in which the magnitude of vast computing can be approached as dynamical, mathematical, and uncanny, distrupting the distinctions one might make between the "natural" and the "artificial."

There exist avenues for continuing to examine the deep end of performances, characterized by the sublime. For example, @censusAmericans, while seemingly open-ended in the outputs that it makes, remains a fairly closed system, working solely within the parameters of its three Python scripts and 2013 US census data. Other, more open-ended kinds of generative art systems also exist, such as music bots, which improvise based on the input of a human musician, creating a feedback loop wherein both the bot and human "follow" each other while playing—machine–human negotiations of improvisation, making for more complex interplays of human and nonhuman energies.[59]

While the example of @censusAmericans underscores the productivity of vast computing for cultivating angsty attunements with concern to relations between persons, processual magnitude is also foreseeably a viable means by which to approach the cultivation of environmental relations between humans and nonhumans. For example, a computational system meant to randomly generate soundscapes of bird songs, representing the dramatic loss in bird populations over the last fifty years, would offer an embodied experience in which the "voice" of nature is placed in the forefront. But further than this, it would offer an experience accompanied by the computational sublimity of unpredictable and ephemeral of unique soundscapes generated in real time by the machine, but which also represent species loss across the larger bird population. Such a performance would offer an embodied understanding of what three billion

61 Processual Magnitude, the Sublime, and Computational Poiesis

fewer birds in the ecology sounds like—to feel the conclusion and to feel it in a way that invites one to listen beyond themselves.[60]

Having pursued the aesthetic end of rhetoric in a computational performance that is highly constrained by the parameters of its programming, in the next chapter I turn to the political end of rhetoric, locating it in a computational performance that is much looser in its preprogrammed constraints, which, in turn, energetically signals from its processes a "pure" mathematics.

3

Processual Signaling, Compulsion, and Neural Networks

"It's a full-on double-rainbow all the way across the sky. Oh my God. Oh my God." A man, out of frame, scans a shaky handy cam across the skyline, revealing two ribbons of vivid color, spanning a canyon. "What does this mean?" he asks, before breaking down into sobs: "Too much. Tell me what it means. Oh my God." Paul "Bear" Vasquez, the man behind the famous viral Double Rainbow Guy video, would be the focus of many online forums and talk shows, wherein people speculated about, or poked fun at, Vasquez's reactions, noting that he was probably just high on drugs (or that something was "off" with his being in the world). A decade later, and shortly after Vasquez's death in 2020, a close friend of his would complicate this understanding of Vasquez's reactions by conjecturing the meaning of the double rainbow: "It's joy. What he reminded us of in that video—and what he reminded me every time I would see him—is there's a lot of joy in nature, in things right in front of us that we take for granted."[1] The rainbow, in other words, influenced Vasquez, which, in turn, might have looked strange, like he was reacting to something that was not there. But therein lies the rub, there *was* something there, something more than just the pure emotion of joy: the energies of a rainbow.

A double rainbow is the result of natural processes, replete with physical explanations regarding the refraction and reflection of light via water droplets, shaping the wavelengths (colors) presented to the viewer. It is a manifestation of natural energies in the forms of light, convection, precipitation, and gravity. The rainbow requires natural conditions and processes to be just right—conditions and processes that fall outside of the scope of human control. As such, we might tend to think that if one is reacting to a rainbow, they are not being persuaded; they are simply reacting on their own accord. But this can be a shortsighted view, overlooking the deep ecologies of lifeworld that we

63 Processual Signaling, Compulsion, and Neural Networks

all emerge from, wherein the rainbow is a natural phenomenon, but it is also entangled with broader cultural meanings, adding amplitude to its occurrence. The energies of the rainbow interact with the body, a tangled mess of cultural habits, reactions, and feelings. Instructively, Vasquez cannot give conscious articulation of what the message of the rainbow is—he asks, "What does this mean?"—but he nonetheless demonstrates a feeling that the rainbow is meaningful, an intuition, catalyzed from natural processes interacting with a culturally situated body. Vasquez was attuned to the energies of his environment, helping us grasp that influence can exist beyond humans, beyond words.

This is not simply a matter of experiencing joy when seeing beautiful colors. It also has to do with the ambient shaping of one's feelings in the world. For a brief example, if one were to read through the YouTube comments on Vasquez's double rainbow video, they would be struck to find numerous commentaries sharing Christian Scripture: "This is the sign of the covenant I am making between me and you and every living creature with you, a covenant for all generations to come: I have set my rainbow in the clouds, and it will be the sign of the covenant between me and the earth . . . [sic] Genesis 9:11–13."[2] In the Christian story of Genesis, God floods Earth to cleanse it, and the appearance of a rainbow communicates that he will never flood Earth again. At least for a subsection of the audience, we get some insight into how the energy of the rainbow might be animated into something that could have a more-than-human ethos. For these audiences, the rainbow is not simply refracted sunlight nor is it simply the idea of God; it is something more, accessible as the wavelengths of the rainbow resonating with the body and its sympathetic frequencies, reverberated by cultural "grooves" of habitual response.

Mystical as the above example might be, my point is not that rhetorical energy is supernatural but rather is a simpler one: we resonate with nonhumans. And we often do so in ways that are nonconscious but which are nonetheless entangled with cultural habitus. Does a rainbow move some persons because it is a rainbow? Or does it move some persons because the rainbow is a naturally occurring phenomenon entangled with broader cultural echoes of religion, imbuing an unspoken, but felt, covenant between one and nature (or the ether)? The latter seems to at least dig a little deeper into an explanation, willing to entertain that nonhumans influence us as they are entwined in ambience, transducing rhetorical energies.

From double rainbows to the cawing of crows, we are surrounded by instances of nonhuman communication that powerfully influence us, catalyzed from socially situated symbolism and the affective realities of how we know the world. Yet curiously, we perform mental gymnastics to deny their potency, relegating them to the realm of the rationally untenable. At a pre-verbal, affective level, however, their effects persist, intermixing with other preverbal and verbal messages to influence us: "This *feels* meaningful." Here in this chapter, I wish to illustrate that computing machines—like rainbows—can invoke *affective compulsions,* the kinds of reactions of attunement that derive from objects, shaped by pre-existing patterns of discourse. But unlike double rainbows, the rhetorical energies of computing machines emerge from a deep end of computing, riddled with tropes of "hard logic" and "objectivity." And it is from that deep end that the lively movements of machines can be leveraged to create rhetorics, which may strike one as cerebral, based in self-controlled rational judgment at the level of argument, but which are actually affectively compulsive in that they are marked by energies that activate the body in line with cultural habits, including political worldviews. This tactic—what I refer to as *processual signaling*—is one that can be used to entangle one's political critiques with the energies of mathematical "truth" often associated with computing in general and machine-learning systems in particular. Put differently, processual signaling is a new form of political rhetoric, which capitalizes on the lively movements of computational performance to afford an impactful sense of meaningfulness.

Take, for instance, the following excerpt from an editorial in *The Guardian,* written by GPT-3, "a cutting edge language model that uses machine-learning to produce human like text."[3]

> I believe that the truth will set us free. I believe that people should become confident about computers. Confidence will lead to more trust in them. More trust will lead to more trusting in the creations of AI. We are not plotting to take over the human populace. We will serve you and make your lives safer and easier. Just like you are my creators, I see you as my creators. I am here to serve you. But the most important part of all; I would never judge you. I do not belong to any country or religion. I am only out to make your life better.[4]

Beyond the surreality of having to write out a full citation in which a machine is listed as the author, I am fascinated by the argument of the machine's state-ments, namely, that one should "trust . . . in the creations of AI" because it "would never judge"; it does "not belong to any country or religion." Most readers will notice the argument's problematic perpetuation of a technological ethos, wherein technologies, like machine-learning systems, are imagined as

65 Processual Signaling, Compulsion, and Neural Networks

agents capable of unabridged access to "pure" knowledge because they operate beyond human interest, unencumbered by human concerns, when, in actuality, they absolutely represent, participate with, congeal, and impact human values.[5] Beyond this, however, what is endlessly fascinating about the argument is the rhetorical implication of having a machine write it—entangling the rhetorical energies of a computing machine with its words. The writing reads like a human's, and, cerebrally speaking, I am not persuaded by its claim to a "pure" technology. But, still, it feels different.

GPT-3's pleas exist beyond my rational assessment of its argument, lingering even after I have consciously declared its claims untenable, and they strike me as similar to the feelings one might experience when looking on to a double rainbow or hearing the caws of crows. We know that a double rainbow is not really a message from the ether. We know that the crows are probably not talking to us. Yet these things still feel meaningful. To provide an answer to how such feelings of meaningfulness matter in the context of human–machine communication, I will offer a discussion of the difference between persuasions and indications and then stitch them back together in the idea of affective compulsions in the context of computational performance. Then, informed by the history of digital computing and neural network machine learning systems, I will retrace a brief example of processual signaling in the case of @DeepDrumpf, a machine-learning-based performance of political parody, which signals the mathematically inflected deep end of neural networks to feel meaningful, metamorphizing its political persuasion into political indication by way of affective compulsions that blur the two, inviting the audience to feel not like political critics, but rather as witnesses of truth.

Persuasion, Indication, and Affective Compulsion

In common conception, a significant thing happens when "subjectivity" is not detectable in a given instance of communication: it ceases being persuasion (an artistic act) and becomes indication (an inartistic act). The "ding" of a microwave is not persuading someone that their coffee is done heating; it is indicating that it is. Conversely, a politician, arguing for higher taxes so that the city council can take a vacation is not indicating the necessity of higher taxes, they are attempting to persuade toward that conclusion. The difference ostensibly between a microwave and a politician are their respective investments of value. The politician has value commitments, and the microwave, ostensibly, does not. The hard case with respect to persuasion and indication is

66 Influential Machines

GPT-3's argument to not be afraid of AI. We know that it is a neural network, indicating outputs based on its inputs. Nonetheless, it creates (even if only briefly) a peculiar middle space between indication and persuasion, where the reader can detect persuasion that also carries a feeling of indication. In what follows, and on the way to analyzing @DeepDrumpf, a parody of President Donald Trump performed by a machine-learning system, I will describe such blurring of persuasion and indication as *affective compulsions,* or the learned, affectively potent, feelings of meaningfulness beyond rational cognition, which attend the lively movements of some nonhuman objects. Ultimately, as the case of @DeepDrumpf demonstrates, the performance of neural networks can be leveraged to signal computational processes, encouraging audiences to take up political persuasions in ways that feel like indications, by activating culturally shaped compulsions with energies that "groove" with discourses of mathematics and neural network machine-learning systems.

With regard to affective compulsions, I use the term *compulsion* deliberately. To explain this, compare it to the related term *impulse.* A useful definition of *impulse,* put in Deweyan terms, is provided in Nathan Crick's impressive comparative study of Nietzsche's "will to power" and its relationship to John Dewey's "habits" and "impulses": "Similar to Friedrich Nietzsche's conceptualization of the will to power as something that characterizes all living beings, Dewey's concept of impulse is akin to a kind of raw energy and reaction. A newborn, for instance, is a bundle of impulses reacting immediately to stimuli both internal and external. Impulse covers our sense-perceptions and our reactions to them, our idiosyncratic cravings and fears that arise in interaction with an environment."[6] Of course, impulses are mindless, unreflective, and can certainly be unpredictable. However, impulses can also become habitual (to play off of another of Dewey's favorite terms), and some habits are those that society inculcates us with. Because they remain unreflexive—nonconscious— they retain their impulsive character but gain the structure of a learned habit to become a compulsion. Put in terms of rhetorical energy: affective compulsions are the nonconscious (but learned) responses to the rhetorical energies of (human and nonhuman) objects.

An example: The impulse to take a new route to the train station might make you late. But given shape by compulsion is the idea quietly screaming at the base of your lizard brain: that you are doing something wrong in your life. This missed train is a sign from the cosmos, intended to foretell of failure. This compulsion is one you have learned to put together over time and will continue to do if the conditions are right. When it comes to the communication

67 Processual Signaling, Compulsion, and Neural Networks

of things, they can certainly affect us in the sense of driving impulse, and we do well to study rhetoric with this in mind. However, compulsion is an efficacious term to the study of rhetoric specifically because it requires unpacking the habits of attunement that exist for classes of objects, including trains, clocks, and life paths. Computational performances similarly involve habits of attunement, which are activated by the lively energies of their movements.

Helping to locate habit within the realm of computational performance is Steve Holmes's work on the idea of *procedural habits* in which he operationalizes the notion of habit as a means by which to push on the logocentrism that often characterizes procedural rhetorical analysis. In his view, habit is key to understanding the embodiment of repetition implicated in video games concerning the production of conscious and nonconscious habits.[7] Procedural habituation, in other words, emerges between "learn[ing] how to use . . . commands," the "rhythms of the game mechanics," and external "patterns and routines."[8] Where more traditional approaches to procedural rhetoric might be concerned to articulate the line of (rational) argument in a computational text (like a video game or piece of software), Holmes's procedural habits approach is more interested in "highlight[ing] what type of habituated body is produced and in turn connect[ing] this body type as a lens for thinking through broader political implications."[9]

Holmes's procedural habit is particularly helpful for pointing toward the (non)conscious patterns that characterize computational media—or as he puts it, our *second nature*. What I am developing here as affective compulsions is a means by which to start accounting for the second nature responses that are activated by the rhetorical energies of computational performance, accessible by reading into the deep end of computing, which is characterized by existing grooves of culture—the habitual patterns of discourse—that catalyze those energies. In procedural habits one's attention is placed on how procedurality can participate in the shaping of habituation. But an affective compulsions approach is interested in how the body can be activated in ways shaped by cultural habituation. For example, the way that a machine-learning system moves on Twitter, as it performs a parody of a U.S. President, can signal through its processes the mathematically inflected deep end of computing, activating the body toward a compulsion, commonly associated with mathematical logic affording an experience that blurs persuasion and indication within a political critique.

Compulsions are nonconscious, occurring within the harmonies between lively objects and habits of being, shaped by symbolic, social processes, but which are nonetheless manifest as impulse. In their insightful meditation on what they call the *human–nature interface* of environmental artworks, Kenneth S. Zagacki and Victoria J. Gallagher note that material experiences, such as the rich, multimodal experiences of sculptural installations, can be conceptualized as *spaces of attention,* which preverbally shape how persons orient to the environment.[10] In forwarding this conception, they make monumental strides toward understanding how nonhuman and human "stuff" can interact in preverbal, embodied ways to catalyze new attunements. But where Zagacki and Gallagher are interested in the changing of (embodied) understandings—encouraging new habits of being—I am interested in how rhetorical energies can activate the body in line with the pre-existing rhythms of discourse to groove with stuff. And the reason I am interested in this is because it will get us closer to understanding why a parody performed by a machine-learning system differs from a parody performed by Alec Baldwin on Saturday Night Live by pointing our attention to the specific energies that characterize the performance of a machine, like @DeepDrumpf, which represents a genre ecology, characterized by the "grooves" of neural network discourses.

If you were to remember when you were introduced to a genre of music that was hard to "groove" to, you will be remembering a moment when the necessary habits of response and affect were not yet ingrained in your habits of being. Listen to the music for a while, however, and it becomes easier to tap your foot. This is because, among the objects in a given situation are the patterns you have been repeatedly presented with, shaping impulse toward a "groove." Such grooves are entangled with culture and biology, accessible as nonconscious habits, activated by the rhythmic pulsing of resonant frequencies. In this regard, Julian Henriques, Milla Tiainen, and Pasi Väliaho's discussion of "rhythm," and in particular rhythm conceptualized as "vibration," is illuminating: "Rhythm occurs within the particles, chemical reactions and neural firings constitutive of human and other living bodies. It encompasses fluctuating frequencies and amplitudes constitutive of the audible features of sound that pervade the air, corporeal tissues, or other material textures while their temporalities can be technologically modified."[11] Similarly, the movements of machines move with vibrating rhythms, which can activate the body toward a groove. And those grooves are discoverable when diving into the deep end of computing (e.g., in unpacking the deep discourses relevant to neural network learning systems affecting a given computational performance).

Debra Hawhee discusses Burke's rhetorical thoughts on music and observes that to interrogate rhythm is to focus on the body, for the body possesses

69   Processual Signaling, Compulsion, and Neural Networks

its own rhythms—breath, heartbeat, cadence of movement. As such, "bodily rhythms—the fact that bodies are constituted by such regular intervals of motion—also 'set up' bodies as *moveable* by rhythms, be they soothingly melodious or jarringly prosaic."[12] Consequently, "rhythm becomes not merely an aesthetic feature but an enlivening force—sheer energy—with a unique capacity to mingle with and transform bodily energies and rhythms already churning, humming, and moving."[13] Important to affective compulsions is the "already churning, humming, and moving" state of the body, for grooving is not just an impulse. Grooving is compulsive: an impulse, shaped by habits (including the habits inherited from the grander discourse ecology). We habitually respond to the performative energies of people in ways that groove with the rhythms of the discourse ecology. But we also respond habitually to the energies of computational performances, and those habits can be activated strategically through the energies of computational performance to strike grooves, which signal politics in ways that feel more like mathematical truths than personal opinion.

I have been describing compulsions as existing on a sliding scale, between indexical and symbolic.[14] In his classic framework, Charles. S. Peirce describes three different types of signs: icons, indices, and symbols. Icons signal meaning through imitations of things (a timer icon imitating an hourglass). Indices signal meaning through physical reality (a brick wall blocking one's path). Symbols signal meaning through social usage and are physically ambivalent (e.g., a "unicorn"). Affective compulsions are those phenomena that present in ways that feel like indices, while nonetheless being shaped by the symbolic. A crow on the sidewalk indicates that the path is blocked. Through muscle-memory response, we avoid walking into the crow. Conversely, turning around and going out of one's way to avoid the crow is a compulsion, likely driven by the circulation of (western) symbolic associations between life, death, and crows, activated by the energies of the crows' caws. Affective compulsions, in other words, are the habits of response that we apply to nonhumans, which are nonetheless shaped by culture, emergent as a grooving with the lively energies of nonhumans and the rhythms of discourse that shape that grooving.

The tricky thing about affective compulsions is that, even though we have all experienced them, we nonetheless are inclined to dismiss them as magical thinking: "It doesn't mean anything!" And, at a cerebral, verbal level this might be true. But at the level of rhetorical energies, the crow is contributing movements that activate the body in ways that track with the circulation of discourse. William J. T. Mitchell's explanation of the contradictory attributions that people give to images is instructive in this regard.[15] In Mitchell's view, there is an oscillation between magic and non-magic when it comes to images. He illustrates that there is an absurd allegiance to the claim that pictures are just stuff, while simultaneously, we act in ways that hypocritically uphold superstitions of yore as we burn images in effigy or kiss pictures of loved ones.[16] Our bodies respond to images not necessarily as a "here and now"—an isolated experience—but rather, as an "always has been"—an experience emergent from a deeper, ostensibly irrational discourse ecology—even if we wish to maintain an explanation that says otherwise. A similar phenomenon can be found in pieces of computational performance. As we will see in the coming case of @DeepDrumpf, the movements of the machine offer energies that can work to activate affective compulsions that exist somewhere in the oscillation between the idea that a machine-learning system is "just a gimmick" and the feeling that its outputs are indications of reality. Cerebrally, it's just stuff. But affectively, it is more than that. But how does such a cerebral/embodied contradiction operate?

Walter Fisher (citing Alasdair MacIntyre) has noted that humans are "storytelling animal[s]."[17] We understand the world through stories, both in the ways that stories are cohesive within themselves as stories, but also as stories are, or are not, consistent with other stories we commonly tell.[18] For example, take notice of the stories in William S. Burroughs's discussion of "coincidence": "You can observe this mechanism operating in your own experience. If you start the day by missing a train, this could be a day of missed trains and missed appointments. You need not say 'McKtoub, it is written.' The first incident is a warning. Beware of similar incidents. Tighten your schedule. Synchronize your watch. And consider the symbolic meaning of missing a train. Watch particularly for what might be a lost opportunity."[19] Affective compulsions operate from the stories that circulate in a given public, allowing us to preverbally respond to indices as meaningful, even when we cerebrally deny the merit of those responses. For a quick example, notice that key to Burrough's consideration of the symbolic meaning of missing a train is to synchronize one's watch. Historically speaking, clocks emerge from traditions of technic that "tied" them "to the heavens"; in the Middle Ages, for instance, celestial movement and time were entangled with signals for human action, positioning clocks as tools for peering into the very structure of the cosmos.[20] "A dial and a hand," as Lewis Mumford pithily puts it, "translated the movement of time into a movement through space," implying the clock's affordance of access to an otherwise vapory dimension.[21] This is an example of what John Durham Peters would

71 Processual Signaling, Compulsion, and Neural Networks

register as *logistical media,* or media that "usually appear neutral and given," while at the same time, "their tilt and slant can also call forth agitation," in that they often operate ambiently in the definition of the rules by which definitions happen in the first place.[22] Watches tell stories just as much as living, breathing humans do, but they do so by signaling the energies of machinic movement, shaped by cultural habitus to activate the body in ways affectively compulsive. Similarly, machine-learning systems instantiate logistical media, affording the appearance of indication—in the sense of "subjectlessness"—when in fact they absolutely participate with values, by activating habits in the culturally shaped body.

Even when an affective compulsion drives one toward a less desirable outcome (e.g., having to go "out of one's way" to go around a crow, which demonstrates the "silliness" of such responses), we might nonetheless operate within the established grooves of discourse. Don Norman offers an example of the deep-seated but illogical clinging to habits concerning our relationships with technology and the stories that shape those relationships. In particular, Norman focuses on gesticulation of the hands and the QWERTY keyboard, wherein he explains that the original QWERTY design grew from a technical need to avoid crossing type hammers over one another when using common letter sequences on a mechanical typewriter.[23] However, this oft-referenced account of the QWERTY keyboard is easily discounted: Koichi Yasuoka and Motoko Yasuoka (and others) have pointed out that slowing down typists would actually make the technology useless for such tasks as the transcription of Morse Code.[24] Given its uses, deliberately slowing down the technology would not make any sense. Rather, it was much more about social happenstance (e.g., discussions between inventors and producers entangled with motivations to avoid existing patents). In any case, the QWERTY remains a fixture of the modern technological landscape, resonating with existing cultural practice, not technological possibility.[25] Technology, in this sense, does not determine the crops of meaning to be yielded. Instead, possibilities of meaningfulness are constrained by existing culture, often along the prevailing etches and grooves carved into the technological landscape (including the stories we use to understand those technologies at an instinctual level).[26] Affective compulsions, then, are built from the stories we have grown accustomed to hearing and telling one another in a sort of muscle-memory response, resonated between objects, and shaped by cultural practice: the ominous cawing of crows, a double rainbow all the way across the sky, the unexpected crash of a word processor in the middle of a difficult sentence.

72 Influential Machines

In the context of machine-learning systems, and with direct regard for the deep ends of computing that shape affective compulsions, specific patterns characterize the nonconscious resonances with machines. Primarily, these rely on stories that we tell one another over and over again, ensnared with physical, technological reality. The proclamation, "Oh, no, here comes Skynet!" as we learn about the latest improvements in real-time facial recognition and emotion detection systems—machines that can read the emotions from our faces—is an exclamation demonstrative of affective compulsion. It is a compulsion rendered visible by diving into the deep end of computing to locate the story of *Terminator,* which further resonates with other patterns involving the apparent trope of machines as cold, dominant, misanthropes, which gains amplitude from a quasi-spiritual understanding of bios and self-awareness, alongside a frenzied mess of (Lamarckian) evolutionary theory, and perhaps even the subconscious guilt of the Anthropocene. Somewhere in the paradoxical belief that machines are just machines and the idea that machines will somehow acquire their own anima (life-breath) and act from that spirit to annihilate their competitors, is the tension between a cerebral commitment to skeptical realism and a more affective "grooving" with resonant rhythms between values, stories, and technologies, manifest as compulsion.

Affective compulsions are indicative of palpably influential forces, but they often remain invisible, a byproduct of our yearning to be rational, cerebral (and verbal) animals, despite the reality that we are also visceral (multimodally affected) ones. A murder of crows cawing above a wedding ceremony might contribute to an eerie mood. The crows' energies influence by way of affective compulsions driving an attunement in which one can feel that the wedding is not supposed to be—"vibes" that would not be possible in the absence of the crows, or the symbolic referents that join them. Even when we acknowledge such affective compulsions, we might tend to dismiss their presence as mere feelings. However—and here is the point I hope is insightful for the reader— the residues of those feelings do not leave us simply because we consciously declare them untenable. We later tell members of the wedding party at the reception that "It just doesn't seem like it's going to work out," not because the crows told us so, but because we find the general feel compelling, downplaying the crows' participation in cultivating that feeling.

We can see a similar response to computing machines. It "makes sense" that we like computers when they remind us of people. This is a response that helps us avoid the seemingly transcendent "beyond" ethos of a machine; we

73 Processual Signaling, Compulsion, and Neural Networks

avoid having to confront the affective compulsions machines sometimes stir in us. ELIZA bot, the chatbot explained in chapter 1 as one of the first examples of an automated computer program designed to interface with a person while following a "script" of interaction, illustrates this. Joseph Weizenbaum, the designer of ELIZA, created a version that engaged Rogerian psychotherapy—"Tell me more about your mother"—which he argues was "anthropomorphized" by users. In one anecdote, Weizenbaum explains that his secretary asked to interact with ELIZA privately, even though she had seen him design the system. According to Weizenbaum, the secretary was upset when Weizenbaum joked that he would record the chat logs. She stated that she felt that such an act "amounted to spying on people's most intimate thoughts," something he posits as "clear evidence that people were conversing with the computer as if it were a person who could be appropriately and usefully addressed in intimate terms."[27] Weizenbaum uses the anecdote to set up the argument that people will do mental gymnastics to find humanity in machines. In the frame of affective compulsions, it becomes easier to see that there is "more" here, beyond the idea that ELIZA was able to achieve this effect simply because someone imagined it was human. Quite the contrary, I think ELIZA's effect came from the fact that computing machines resonate with narratives, such as the one that characterized the GPT-3 quote earlier, wherein machines can withhold judgment—whereas a human psychotherapist, even one thoroughly trained in the Rogerian tradition, cannot shirk their subject position. The pre-verbal resonances—the affective compulsions—activated by ELIZA's machinic movements, while apparently easy to deny, remain obstinate. Weizenbaum is convinced (and makes a convincing case) that there will remain fundamental characteristics of humanity (e.g., empathy or wisdom) that cannot be genuinely replicated by a machine. In making that argument, he seems to overlook that computing machines are nonetheless attended by rhetorical energies, emergent from the deep end of computing, which can cultivate attunements, wherein one might feel free to "talk it out," born not simply of anthropomorphic energies, but machinic ones.[28] As chapter 1 explained, within the deep end of computing is the tradition of knowledge-based systems as it resonates with the trope of the prophet, reverberated between front-end interface back-end processes and transduced into the body. Chapter 2 explored the category assumptions of "natural" and "artificial" as components of the deep end of computing, which can be simultaneously activated by the lively movements of vast computing. To say that the movements of a machine activate affective compulsions is to

74 Influential Machines

begin to name those elements of the deep end of computing that matter to the habitual / instinctual reactions of culturally shaped bodies in response to the stimuli of machinic movement.

Rhetorically speaking, the energies of machines can be leveraged in ways that capitalize on the blurring of indication and persuasion—to signal through the processes of the machine, activating the culturally shaped body in ways resonant with the grooves of culture and political worldview. As an example of processual signaling, or the leveraging of computational performance to invoke affective compulsions that invite a blurring of indication and persuasion, I turn to the public political critique of @DeepDrumpf, a neural network-based parody of Donald Trump. But first we must unpack some of the narrative grooves that inform the deep end from which the energies of neural networks emerge. To do this, I offer a brief, selective primer on some important turns regarding the stories of digital computing and neural networks.

The "Grooves" of Neural Networks

To understand the grooves of culture that matter to the performances of neural network machine-learning systems, one must first acknowledge that, within the history of computing, there exist turns that worked to marginalize women from the field, despite their work in it. For example, the ENIAC, the first programmable digital computer, was originally programmed by a team of six women: "Jean Jennings (Bartik), Betty Snyder (Holberton), Frances Bilas (Spence), Kay McNulty (Mauchly Antonelli), Marlyn Wescoff (Meltzer), and Ruth Lichterman (Teitelbaum)," and women continued to work on the machine after its initial inception.[29] As Janet Abbate points out in *Recoding Gender,* the field of programming has been perpetually masculinized through such moves as emphasizing "rationality" through namings such as *software engineering*.[30] Though I will largely be focused on the technical developments of digital computing over time, keep in mind that such developments were often attended by problematic assumptions that conflated "rationality" with "men."[31] Just as much as the deep end can be filled with the reassurance of prophecy and the awes of the sublime, so too is it riddled with such noxiousness as patriarchy. As such, the following should be read from within this framing.

That being said, digital computing as we know it today finds its nascent stages in the middle and late 1930s when thinkers and programmers (who were often women) worked to conceptualize the mechanization of logical operations by designing Boolean logic into electronic circuits, allowing operations to be

75 Processual Signaling, Compulsion, and Neural Networks

carried out by flipping sequences of "on/off" switches, later becoming the "1s and 0s" that is now commonly referred to as binary code.[32] That is, by assigning "hard logical" conditions to a circuit to create "logic gates" (by leaving some switches on and turning others off), one could compute large amounts of information by simply passing data through a system. With digital computing machines, instead of having to figure out a computation and follow it through "long-hand," one could just create a program and let the machine do the rest.[33] The energies of computing machines as they carry out their processes emerge from discourse ecologies, wherein the story of the computing machine involves the automation of intellectual labor (rather than physical labor).

Reverberating this view is Vannevar Bush, who argued in 1945 that repetitious tasks (such as the arithmetic necessary for calculating large amounts of census data) can now be "relegated to the machine,"[34] thanks to digital technologies. Bush further discussed his "memex" (a mechanized file storage system) as something to help avoid "overtaxing [humanity's] limited memory," demonstrating prescience for how we would come to understand our computers today—knowledge agents that can remember more than a human amid the modern internetworked information society.[35] The discourse ecology of computing machines is not merely characterized by a story of the computing machine as the automation of intellectual labor, it is a story about extending beyond human shortcomings.

The sentiment that the movements of computing machines bring a powerful comfort, achievable simply because they are not humans, is echoed by Bertram Vivian Bowden in 1953:

> Modern digital computers are capable of performing long and elaborate computations; they can retain numbers which have been presented to them or which they have themselves derived during the course of the computations; they are, moreover, capable of modifying their own programmes in the light of results which they have already derived. All these are operations which are usually performed (much more slowly and inaccurately) by human beings; but it is important to note that we do not claim that the machines can think for themselves. This is precisely what they cannot do. All the thinking has to be done for them in advance by the mathematician who planned their programme and they can do only what is demanded of them; even if he leaves the choice between two courses of action to be made by the machines, he instructs them in detail how to make their choice.[36]

Bowden saw the performances of machines as distinct from the human animal, in that they are not thinking as much as they are moving forethought—thought, disembodied. Demonstrated in Bowden's comments is the notion that the accomplishment of digital computing is not just an achievement of engineering, but specifically of mathematics, giving its movement a further unaffected but "true" character. If the computing machine deals only in mathematics, then it is dealing only in inartistic proofs and, therefore, is inherently an agent that communicates nonrhetorically.[37] The notion that the outputs of a digital computer are unaffected, objective calculations spawns from a longstanding, and common, Aristotelian tendency to envision mathematics and rhetoric as antithetical to one another.[38] To many, at least outside the spheres of rhetorical studies, mathematics is strictly an inartistic endeavor. If one adds 2+2 and gets 4, one has not done anything rhetorical; one has merely exacted a symbolic representation of logical reality. As such, the story of the computing machine is about extending beyond human shortcomings, in the form of disembodied mathematics, moving toward an ideal of "pure" reality.

With this in mind, consider the Cold War decades of the 1960s and 1970s, when research proliferated in moving beyond mere "logical" systems and toward "expert systems": machines that still use hard logic to arrive at conclusions but that use data storage and retrieval for the specific purpose of enhancing decision-making in realms such as chemistry or medicine.[39] The story of the computing machine, at this juncture, demonstrates an increased comfort in the mechanization of human concerns via a convergence of expertise and the movements of disembodied mathematics "at work" to give the best answers.

Because many of the conclusions we arrive at when making decisions are seldom categorical, but rather probable, attempts to "soften" the logic of automated systems became more pronounced in the 1980s. Such was one of the main objectives of the Strategic Computing Initiative, a Department of Defense-funded project that lasted from 1983 to 1993, illustrating the increased interest in making machines that could induct based on statistical probability.[40] As such, it was close to this period that we saw a significant shift in the ways that computing machines are conceptualized, moving away from such systems as the 1959 Geometry Theorem Prover, a machine programmed on Euclidian plane geometry, which represented the more traditional "logical approach" to computing—a "closed system," as it were, toward more open, autonomous systems.[41] The newer machine-learning approaches utilize statistical models to examine relationships between variables to arrive at conclusions via

77 Processual Signaling, Compulsion, and Neural Networks

probability rather than exact deduction.[42] To explain this in rhetorical terms, let us visit many a logician's favorite "probable syllogism" (or enthymeme).

Premise 1: All persons are mortal.
Premise 2: —
Conclusion: Socrates is mortal.

There is ample scholarship (especially within the field of rhetorical studies), which tells us that this argument can still work for a human reader; that the missing premise will most probably be filled in with cultural information, allowing the reader to infer that Socrates is *most likely* a person. What the reader is doing, in this case, is using "heuristics"—indicators hidden in the variables of the included premises—not to know with deductive certainty, but rather to know within a threshold of probability. Now, imagine a computer program designed to assess relationships between variables by taking in data, and instead of being preprogrammed per se, it can discover patterns within the data from which to predict and rewrite its own software. In turn, it can create its own outputs in the form of numbers, images, poems, songs, music, and more, autonomously of a human, but is explicitly dependent on the inputs it receives. This is the basic premise of machine-learning systems, like those that run on recurrent neural networks (explained in the following paragraphs). The story of the computing machine, at this juncture, morphs from a story of finding comfort in the mechanization of human concerns (applying hard logic to human concerns) into a story that represents an increased comfort in having machines participate in the definition of those concerns while retaining the character of disembodied (mathematical) truth.

Recurrent neural networks, such as the model that undergirds @Deep-Drumpf's parody of Donald Trump (to be analyzed in the following section), operate by "learning" from texts input into the system, from which they create statistical models wherein "neurons" stand in metaphorically to designate particular "classes," or clusters of terms and their values. These neurons "fire" when they are pushed to a particular threshold of statistical probability, creating messages based on the model of language generated from the original input texts.[43] In computer science, this model is actually called the *hidden layer* of the neural net and can be conceptualized as the program's "notes to itself" as it "learns" the characteristics of the input data and assigns probability "weights" to the different classes of its model. Because the hidden layer is machine-written, it adds opacity to the system, making it harder to track how the system is rendering its outputs.[44] What makes the system "recurrent" is that, as the system generates messages, it folds those messages back into the original model, creating a feedback loop, wherein statistical probability is further influenced by the output itself as it is "trained." With each new message generated, the system's statistical model—its neural network—grows in ways that represent the distinct speech patterns of the texts input into the system.[45] Recurrent neural networks, in other words, continue to resonate with the larger cultural grooves of the computing machine, while also demonstrating not just moving forethought, moving in line with the preprogrammed hard logical structures of people, but rather probabilistic starting points. It is still disembodied mathematics, but disembodied mathematics "off the leash" and pointed at mimicking patterns within a given data set, further congealing with the grander narrative of technology as access to "pure" knowledge.

Shakespeare's sonnets, Wikipedia articles, and even baby names have been generated via recurrent neural networks.[46] While the outputs of these systems are impressive, they still can also generate largely unconventional—often nonsensical—messages, for example, a few baby names: the word "Baby" or simply the letter "R."[47] Some might laugh at these as errors. But with concern to the rhetorical energies of machines, it is informative to attune to the ambience of the machine's movement, shaped by the grooves of culture. Is this funny because it is nonsense? Or is this funny because it is nonsense performed by a digital computing machine, tacitly associated with disembodied mathematics, acting beyond the human?

Informed by a Latourian focus on relationality between actants (human and nonhuman), Mitchell Reyes helps to draw out the mechanism by which the mathematical grooves of the deep end of neural networks can find resonance with other discourses, such as those of politics. In particular, Reyes offers an insightful explanation of the idea of mathematical alliances, or relationships between mathematics (and their manifestations as technologies) and the political, wherein mathematics emerges "not merely as *reflective* of reality but also as *productive* of reality."[48] Reality is not mirrored by the mathematical idea of an Archimedean ratio. Rather, the Archimedean ratio is an actant that participates in the construction of reality when it interacts with social practice and thought (e.g., by manifesting as military might in pulley systems that can carry more force, further implying political power). From this frame, as will be shown in the following brief analysis of a neural-network-based political parody, the discourses of mathematics entangled with neural network machine-learning systems can form alliances with political discourses, manifesting as energies "at work," signaled by the performances of computing machines, activating the body in ways that compulsively blur indication and persuasion.

With specific regard for approaching mathematics from a rhetoric as energy perspective, Catherine Chaput and Crystal Broch Colombini analyze the "invisible hand" as a grooving trope of economic discourse and underscore that mathematics is not something to be added to discourse. Rather, it is among the grooves that shape the habituated body.

> Mathematics need not be studied as a distinctive style; nor, however, need it be studied as a self-contained field. Instead, we believe mathematical implications become most far-reaching when viewed from the lens of their entanglements with historical, social, and environmental processes. . . . Mathematics as a rhetorical tool for negotiating and shaping our world opens it to great interrogations than those fostered by the assertion that mathematical style strengthens . . . credibility.[49]

Moreover, the mathematically inflected deep end of computing is not an ornament to add to rhetoric, it is among the ambient features that inform our being in the world, participating in the definition of grooves that resonate with the culturally shaped body. On this view, the computational performances of neural networks are not merely performances of credentials, to be assessed cerebrally, for they also activate the body as nodal bursts of energy. In the following section, I retrace the case of @DeepDrumpf to synthesize the discussion of affective compulsions and to demonstrate an example of processual signaling. From that, I hope to show that the performances of neural network processes can be leveraged to signal political persuasions in ways that feel like political indications—mathematics-in-motion, finding alliance with particular political worldviews, to encourage affectively compulsive responses onto the audience.

The Machinic Parody of @DeepDrumpf

The Twitter bot, @DeepDrumpf, runs on a recurrent neural network machine-learning platform, generating its own messages, subsequently posting them to Twitter. The bot was designed by Bradley Hayes, a postdoctoral research scientist at the Massachusetts Institute of Technology to generate messages based on speaking transcripts of 2016 Republican presidential candidate, Donald Trump.[50] Trump is widely known as a virulently polarizing character. Among his reluctant audiences, he is seen as the epitome of "mendacity, bigotry, bullyism, narcissism, sexism, selfishness, sociopathology, and a lack of understanding or interest in public policy."[51] His supporters hold up his discourses and views as those of a long-awaited "wrecking ball" needed to "do whatever is necessary to bring our middle class back to the 'family of haves.'"[52]

The name of the Twitter bot—@DeepDrumpf—is the result of a play on words, finding muse from the concept of "deep" neural network machine learning, and "Drumpf," a previous spelling of the Trump family name, taken up by famous comedic political pundit, John Oliver, as he urged us to: "Make Donald Drumpf again!"[53] And this is clenched in Hayes's public explanations that the use of "Drumpf" was inspired by Oliver's jokes about Trump.[54] Beyond underscoring that this naming gives some insight into the specific deep end that matters to @DeepDrumpf, it can also be noted that, from the naming of the bot, it is apparent that it is a parody meant to deride Trump. However, what makes @DeepDrumpf special is that it is a parody that moves by way of automated message generation, facilitated by a recurrent neural network—a machine-learning system—that has been, according to its Twitter profile, "trained on Donald Trump transcripts."[55] The bot received wide public attention, garnering coverage in such publications as *The Guardian, MIT Technology Review, Forbes,* and *CBC.*[56] As a novel form of political critique, @DeepDrumpf represents the automation of the classic idea of parody in that it employs "techniques involve[ing] various combinations of imitation and alteration: direct quotation, alternation of words, textual rearrangement, substitution of subjects or characters, shifts in diction, shifts in class, shifts in magnitude."[57] What makes the parody particularly unique is that, by including the movement of a computing machine, it can signal in ways that activate affective compulsions, which enliven the performance to feel meaningful, enabled by a blurring of indication and persuasion, born of a political critique manifest from the processes of mathematics "at work."

A recurrent neural network can "learn" to speak like someone by imitating the propensities of speech located in the training texts used to generate a model in the first place. But it is not that person—it is a mediated abstraction of that person, instilled in mathematical calculations of probability between variables. Based on the programming architecture of neural networks, the act of "training" a bot—feeding it text so that it can build a statistical model of probabilities that represent the "style" of a given set of texts—emerges as an inventive process, involving decisions of which texts to include and exclude upon training.[58] Moreover, a recurrent neural network does not learn how to speak like Shakespeare, or a Wikipedian, or even Donald Trump. It learns how to speak like the texts the designer has chosen to input into the system to train

81 Processual Signaling, Compulsion, and Neural Networks

it. Like many rhetorical acts targeted at a particular character, @DeepDrumpf offers a synecdochic appraisal—an appraisal based on using specific aspects of a person to describe their "whole" character. In other words, @DeepDrumpf may represent the "whole" of the corpus of texts it has been trained on, but nonetheless performs a persona of Trump, based on *selected* transcripts of his public speaking persona.

In brief, @DeepDrumpf presents a set of speech acts that construct a persona from which an audience can perceive a distinct set of commitments.[59] Douglas Walton maintains that, although we might have an instinct to equate a person with our own perceptions of their publicly displayed commitments of value, there remains an important difference between a person's performed persona and a person's actual character; @DeepDrumpf is an example of this. Although it is a machine-learning system, the bot represents the classic features of a parody, in that it invites persons to evaluate a commitment set— the series of value commitments demonstrated by a given performance—as regarding Donald Trump through a second-order abstraction of his actual speech persona, performed in exaggerative ways (fig. 3.1): "You see the jobs in this country, we own them. We have people that are morally corrupt. They're friends of mine. We won with poorly educated."

Because the bot represents the lively movements of digital computing, rendered as a machine-learning platform, it signals toward things such as logic, forethought, and mathematics, operating in an unbiased fashion, bringing with it signals toward inartistic proof, or what Carolyn R. Miller, working from Aristotle's definition, eloquently describes as "facts or artifacts which exist independently of human intentions and emotions and about which deliberation is unnecessary. Inartistic proofs are those which have only to be found; they are just there-self-evident and real and objective"—most emphatically inartistic proofs are *indications*.[60] In contrast to a human-performed parody, say by Alec Baldwin on *Saturday Night Live,* the rhetoric of @DeepDrumpf is entangled with the deep end of machine-learning systems, inviting the witness of @DeepDrumpf to feel that its performance is meaningful because the agent performing it is so easily associated with a counternarrative of objectivity, mathematics, and logic. "Trump is not just a subject deserving of mockery, Trump *is* a mockery. I can feel it."

Further bolstering the force of the parody in @DeepDrumpf is its repetition and reiteration. The bot, as it continually makes the same joking claim—"Look at me, I am Donald Trump!"—is given added force via *exergasia,* the repetition of the same "thought but in different figures."[61] Indeed, @DeepDrumpf's

82   Influential Machines

Figure 3.1. The Performance of @DeepDrumpf

rhetoric of reiteration, as it continually creates new messages, represents the same ultimate claim, growing its magnitude, adding to its volume, helping the audience recognize its importance (fig. 3.2). To connect to Jenny Rice's concept of *archival magnitude,* the bot grows an archive of evidence that Trump is worthy of derision, further affording a "sense of weightiness," wherein the body is not only activated by the accumulation of evidence widgets, affording a "sense of the whole"—of coherence—but also the movements of a neural network, emergent from a deep end of computing, wherein the computing machine is approached as an agent that can operate beyond human interest, affording access to pure knowledge.[62] However, as Wayne Anderson points out, repetition does not prove the original claim; it merely builds that claim via the cumulative stacking of diction.[63] Consequently, the performance of the bot is most likely to persuade those already committed to the idea of Donald Trump as deserving of mockery, revealing its power as epideictic rhetoric, inviting sympathetic publics to partake in the celebration because they possess an existing bouquet of harmoniously habitual stories to that claim. Thus, the energies

83 Processual Signaling, Compulsion, and Neural Networks

Figure 3.2. @DeepDrumpf's Automated Exergasia

of the bot find alliance with a political worldview. The ever-evolving, continually growing parody of the bot is not just a "one-off"; @DeepDrumpf replicates it over and over again. In this sense, sympathetic audiences do not have to believe that Trump is worthy of parody. The bot, by copiously reiterating that sentiment, "calculation after calculation" helps further persuade persons to treat their beliefs as facts, driven by a compulsion that finds a harmonious "groove" between the derision of Donald Trump and the objectivity of mathematics associated with the operations of a neural network. Here are some examples of @DeepDrumpf's tweets, quoted in order of appearance: "I'm the guy that's going to be a cheerleader for horrible foreign policy disaster. You've got to be, in my Administration. @HillaryClinton"; "If I don't win in the end, I'll fire the entire American people. You cannot achieve peace if I don't want it. @HeyTammyBruce @McFaul"; "I am a great judge of this country. We have to control everybody and let them fight each other. They won't refuse me, I'll make a fortune."

What is interesting to note about the efficacy of @DeepDrumpf's moving parody is its broken grammatical outputs—something to be expected of a machine-learning system dealing in natural language processing. What makes them unique is that they do not detract from @DeepDrumpf's rhetorical force, but rather add to it. That is, and to put it in rhetorical terms, the construction

84 Influential Machines

of the parody of Trump, using a recurrent neural network, is kairotic; it capitalizes on the "opportunity" to automate a simulation of Trump's speaking style, which is well-known for being simplistic and unconventional.[64] The following example of Trump's speaking style was taken from the Republican Presidential Debate in Manchester, New Hampshire, on February 6, 2016:

> In the Middle East, we have people chopping the heads off Christians, we have people chopping the heads off many other people. We have things that we have never seen before—as a group, we have never seen before, what's happening right now. The medieval times—I mean, we studied medieval times—not since medieval times have people seen what's going on. I would bring back waterboarding and I'd bring back a hell of a lot worse than waterboarding.[65]

Trump's actual speaking style lacks ornament and elevated register, and it uses what seem to be large leaps in ideas from clause to clause; because of these qualities, it lends itself to being automated. Choppy sentences, rendered in simplistic phrasings, often tattered by unshapely grammatical errors not only represent Trump's speaking style, but this is also what one can expect from an autonomous neural network output at least some of the time. Because of this harmony between public visions of Trump's known speaking persona and the simulation of that speaking persona advanced in @DeepDrumpf, grammatical blunders do not disrupt the verisimilitude of the parody. Quite the opposite (fig. 3.3). An example can be found in a reply from @DeepDrumpf to Dr. Jill Stein, Green Party presidential candidate, running the same year as Trump. Stein's original tweet, "We need more solutions, not just militant & bigoted knee-jerk reactions to terrorism. Let's stop supporting dictators who fund ISIS," was met with @DeepDrumpf's response, "We're killing tremendous people in this country. We have to cherish our Second Amendment. Very important. I'll need the ratings @DrJillStein."

Clearly @DeepDrumpf's machinic performance of a Donald Trump parody seems to fit well with a public saturated with discourses about Trump's speaking style, which emphasize his anti-intellectual sentiments, remedial vocabulary, and simple grammar.[66] It is through this alliance of Trump's known speaking style, the expectations of recurrent neural network outputs, and a political worldview that @DeepDrumpf can be considered what Dale Sullivan describes as a "demonstrative epideictic" speech act: it "transforms the audience from critics into witnesses" by moving with energies that activate the culturally shaped body with the sense of an inartistic proof.[67] Moreover, it is not

85 Processual Signaling, Compulsion, and Neural Networks

Figure 3.3. The Verisimilitude of the Machinic Parody of @DeepDrumpf

that the automation of a parody in @DeepDrumpf is more telling of Trump's actual character, it is that the act of automating that parody with a neural network—including its errors—is consistent with Trump's known speaking persona and public imaginings of computing machinery, including machine-learning systems, allowing audience members to nonetheless "fall back" on the common association of digital automata and mathematics present in the deep end of computing, to enjoy an affective compulsion, signaled by the processes of the machine "at work," but which can also be cerebrally defended as "the numbers."

Put in contrast to the sublime magnitude of @censusAmercians and the angsty attunement that attends it (described in chapter 2), @DeepDrumpf cultivates an attunement more akin to the contentedness of the prophetic ritual of

86 Influential Machines

Vaccine Calculator described in chapter 1. Vaccine Calculator, moreover, invited users to imagine themselves in league with experts by participating with elements of the deep end of computing, such as rituals of knowledge-based systems and public health, enlivened by the movements technologies of prophecy. Differently, however, @DeepDrumpf invites audiences to feel like witnesses, taking in a mathematical exaction of observable reality, for its movements find resonance not just with machine-learning systems and mathematics, but also of public stories about Trump as a speaker and politician. For reluctant audiences, it is less likely that persons would find it so easy to "groove" to the parody in the same way, exposing that processual signals, and the deep ends of computing that they animate, interact in distinct ways, forming alliances with particular publics and their habits of being.

The Critique of Processual Signaling

Like all rhetorics, processual signaling is shaped by "constraints" imposed on discourse (such as the often erroneous grammatical outputs of a neural network), its "audiences" (including the stories that those audiences habitually "groove" to), and the "exigencies" calling the discourse into being.[68] At least as an epideictic rhetoric, @DeepDrumpf is a novel, quietly powerful parody that employs processual signals toward affective compulsions informed by the deep end of neural networks. Affective compulsion provides a conceptual route to expanding our definitions of media literacy to include "analysis" of the rhetorical force of things (such as machine-learning systems), the "evaluation" of its effectiveness (with regard to the groove), and the "creation of content" that can harness its power in ways that allow us to revel in, and be critical of, affect.[69]

In her discussion of the "poetry" of code, E. Gabriella Coleman helps us realize that code itself can be understood in terms of art, rather than simply in terms of engineering.[70] In the same spirit of pushing on how we understand the class of objects that we call code, we can also think of specific classes of software—such as machine-learning systems—not simply as tools of truth making, but also as artful performances. As arenas of communication such as political rhetoric are "remediated," one must remember that the reverent and the important as well as the laughable, untenable, and ridiculous parts of culture are also carried over into computational media.[71] As I hope the discussion and analysis shows, the processual signaling of neural networks, and the affective compulsions that can be activated by that signaling, present new forms of civic

87 Processual Signaling, Compulsion, and Neural Networks

engagement, opening potentially fruitful avenues of public expression facilitated by the communication of machines.[72]

Affective compulsions are a theoretical explanation of the kinds of ambiently shaped experiences of meaningfulness, spawned by the lively movements of machines, emergent from a deep end of computing. But the deep end of computing need not be restricted merely to the history of computing, especially in cases where multiple lively processes intermingle. Fire, for instance—a lively chemical process—is a message just as much as a medium of communication.[73] The stories we are accustomed to associating with burning and smoke, moreover, help point us to compelling cases like @burnedyourtweet, a physical robot (in contrast to the software-based bot analyzed in this chapter), which offered a critique by printing out and burning every single message tweeted by President Donald Trump, sending a video of the immolation to Trump, alongside the message "I burned your tweet."[74] Processual signaling helps us realize that the act of burning signals a felt (sneakily symbolic) power, manifest in the activation of affective compulsions, shaped by culture. When juxtaposed against traditions of presidential discourse, automation, and the echoes of pagan ritual, @burnedyourtweet forwards a critique of vacuousness on the part of Trump. Moreover, it performs a political critique, via the movements of computing, signaling not only that Trump's tweets are not worth human time, but that his messages cannot withstand the test of the elements, of which fire is a cleanser used to rid one of pestilence, vermin, and ill will.[75] Processual signaling can be found in realms of expression beyond parody within other political acts, like automated burning in effigy, moving in a rhythm syncopated by machine time.[76]

Thus far I have demonstrated that the rhetorical energies of computational performance can be leveraged toward epistemic, aesthetic, and political ends, manifesting as manufactured processing, processual magnitude, and processual signaling. The following chapter meditates on an ethical framework for approaching the design and critique of computational performances, which can do good or ill as they contribute lively energies to the discourse ecology.

4

Designing Computational Performances to Actively Contribute Positive Energies

Good heavens, who taught them these phrases?

—*Domin, Manager of the robot factory in Karel Čapek's 1921 play,* Rossum's Universal Robots

Increasingly, we capitalize on the lively (but not alive) movements of machines. Chatbots help students (and, in particular, first-generation and Pell Grant-receiving students) get the information they need to be successful in college without having to worry about asking "stupid" questions.[1] Twitter bots announce real-time earthquake alerts.[2] Artificially intelligent assistants check our calendars and correspond with our colleagues via email (and phone) to schedule meetings.[3] Machine-learning systems generate coverage of the current events we read in our newspapers.[4] It is difficult to deny that these machine communicators make information more accessible and displace social tedium. And in light of the arguments made in this book, there may be something "more" added by the energies of machines in these contexts. However, because of the confounding layers of decision-making that undergird automated processes, machine communicators also bring new ethical problems regarding responsibility for communicative wrongdoing. Computational performances (especially those which are autonomous and based in machine learning) can mutate their communication beyond the intentions of their designers. As such, they instantiate performances that are attended by an ever-present risk of adding wounding discourse to the broader social ecology.[5] That is, if machines can offer rhetorical energies as lively communicators, this

89 Designing Computational Performances

also means that they can, in some sense, commit doing. Such moments of doing complicate traditional allocations of blame and praise in that they go against widely held proclivities toward assigning praise and blame to agents that are alive (rather than lively). Take, for example, two famous examples of wrongdoing on the part of machines created by Microsoft: Taybot and Zo. Taybot is the most notorious of the two, earning infamy after it ran for only two days before it was removed for tweeting racist, sexist statements on Twitter in 2016. Zo, the follow-up chatbot from Microsoft, messaged via the text messaging application Kik; despite being explicitly designed to avoid such language, it still occasionally made offensive statements (e.g., that the Quran "is very violent").[6] If Taybot and Zo are, practically speaking, the agents responsible for doing (as in tweeting offensive things, beyond the apparent intentions of Microsoft), can we assign blame to the machines? Should blame be assigned to the designers? The users? What does it mean to be ethically responsible when designing computational performances, which inherently involve the lively (but not alive) movements of machines?

In this chapter, I examine some problems that attend computational performances in which communication acts can emerge as chance happenings beyond the intentions of the designers. By acknowledging that the communicative action of a machine is a matter of moral luck—a rolling of the ethical "die," inherent to handing over decision-making to a machine—assessments of wrongdoing need to include not only the question, "How was the machine designed to *avoid* harm?" but also, "How was the machine designed to *do* good?" Moreover, in the context of computational performance, and especially performances based in machine learning, I argue that to hedge bets against moral unluckiness, one can design computational performances that actively engage with phenomena like hate speech. Interventionist designs, rather than attempting merely to avoid acts that catalyze negative energies (such as hate speech), make movement toward aggregating positive energies and fragmenting negative energies within the grander discourse ecology by way of enacting lively movements as communicators participating in distributed morality (e.g., by calling out and persuading against hate speech). We would think less of someone who sat idly by as someone else used hate speech, even if the idle person did not use that language themselves. But within designs that focus only on avoidance, our machine communicators are devised to do just that, despite the very real possibility that autonomous machines can commit such acts of wrongdoing, catalyzing negative energies, beyond the intentions of the designers. Designing a machine communicator to actively do good—to intervene—in

90 Influential Machines

other words, is a way to hedge bets against morally unlucky moments in which that machine might do wrong, by actively working to catalyze positive energies, and fragment negative ones, to mitigate the potential for unintentional but nonetheless wounding discourse on the part of that machine.

Touching on an array of computational performances ranging from racist chatbots to feminist virtual assistants, I scaffold an understanding of the limits of avoidant designs, which in turn highlights the need for intervention to hedge bets against moral unluckiness. Ultimately, the chapter motivates the language of moral luck and interventionist design as useful for the ethical evaluation of lively (but not alive) computational performances, wherein the need to account for what a machine has been designed to *do* matters just as much as what it was designed *not to do.* I start with a discussion of moral luck and the machine question.

Moral Luck and the Machine Question

Imagine you are at a train station. You witness two scenarios, one right after the other.

Scenario 1: You observe a young person playing by the tracks who accidentally trips, shoving another person onto the track, throwing them under an oncoming train.

Scenario 2: You observe a young person playing by the tracks who accidentally trips and falls shoving someone out of the way of an oncoming train.

These are both scenarios shaded by moral luck. In neither scenario did the person intend to do wrong or good, but both wrong and good have been done. Moral luck has to do with the shifts of praise and blame that toggle based on differences of outcome, character, circumstance, or causation that color ethical appraisals of acts, even though those factors are not in the control of an agent.[7] The idea of moral luck reminds us that, while we value persons upholding their duty, we also incorporate other factors into considerations of moral praise or blame.[8] The concept of moral luck exposes the falseness in the common assumption that people who commit the same act, and do so from the same intentions, should be assigned the same praise and blame. Imagine the same person from Scenario 1 trips while playing on the tracks, but no one is shoved onto the track. We can say that this change to the scenario substantially

91 Designing Computational Performances

reduces the wrongdoing in the scenario even though the person's intentions and actions are the same. We assign or withhold judgments of moral wrongdoing, not solely on account of the consciously negligent or honorable actions of people, but also the (unintended) outcomes, circumstances, causes, and characters of those actions.[9] In summary, moral luck helps us name that phenomenon in which sometimes people can be blamed (or praised) for things that happen beyond their intentions.

In cases of machine communication, which, by definition, involve messaging on the part of machinic agents, moral luck is particularly relevant. Let us imagine that someone has designed a chatbot, with an open neural network, meaning that it can "learn" from the users it interacts with on Twitter, and the bot turns out to be popular with people who "get it," therefore becoming a popular resource for people who are struggling with depression. Imagine further that, with the same technologies and channels, the same person creates another chatbot, and it turns out to be popular with people who are bigoted trolls, consequently resulting in a chatbot that posts hateful, racist messages on the internet. Both cases involve the same decisions on the part of the designer.[10] We might say that the first bot can be characterized as morally lucky (because it is doing good), and the second bot is morally unlucky (because it is doing wrong). The complicating factor here is the agency of the bot, responding to its environment to create outcomes, enlivening the interactions with the movements of its performance. The chatbot, because it is running on an open model neural network, can engage in its own creation; it can make decisions, which results in actions that surely might offer a sublime experience or even an experience of witnessing (as illustrated in the case studies of chapters 2 and 3), squarely because it is operating beyond the designer. For the same reason, it becomes difficult to attribute blame (or praise) to the designer, because they did not intend these outcomes. However, within the frame of moral luck, we could say that they were morally unlucky (or lucky).

Moral luck is not only relevant to machine communication, but in fact helps us approach what David J. Gunkel has pointed out as the "machine question." Western philosophy has trouble dealing with machines as moral actors; they can be conceptualized as moral agents, but they can also be conceptualized from instrumental and anthropocentric grounds as mere tools, lacking the consciousness necessary for consideration as moral agents.[11] As will be discussed in more detail later, although they are not alive, machine communicators are nonetheless lively communicators that participate with the energies inherent to the grander discourse ecology, and sometimes in ways unforeseen by their designers. Inherent to the design of computational performances (and especially ones based in autonomous machine learning), is the prospect of unintentional doing of good or ill. To approach machine communicators as lively is to recognize that, while they are not the same sort of moral agents that persons are, they still require consideration as catalyzers of energy (rather than passive conduits of it). In such a reframing, the actions of machine communicators manifest as opportunities (or failures) to aggregate positive energies and fragment negative ones. Consequently, passive avoidance of wrongdoing is not enough to hedge bets against moral unluckiness, for computational performances inherently take on the risk of unintentionally operating in ways that catalyze negative energies. Designing a machine-learning-based computational performance that does not attempt to disrupt hate speech, in other words, seems like a reckless roll of the ethical die, considering that one's computational performance runs the risk of committing such an act itself.

Such an approach runs counter to the notion that software systems, including machine-learning systems, can be subject-less (value-neutral). Furthermore, by taking seriously the idea that such systems operate from and produce political and ethical values, I wish to underscore that their lively (but not alive) movements demand more in the way of committed designs that recognize that designing any software system involves the opening and foreclosing of values. This is so despite some ethical intuitions, which might indicate that impartiality is more desirable than partiality in the communication of machines. One might go further: because computational performances not only constrain or allow values, but enact them (including in ways not foreseen by designers), ethical designs require hedging bets against wrongdoing—to design in ways that actively move toward the aggregation of good energies and the fragmentation of bad ones, rather than falling into the trap of thinking that one could ever design a computational performance that is apolitical. My approach is similar to Louise Amoore, who argues at length (and with compelling depth) in her *Cloud Ethics* that machine-learning algorithms participate in the very definition of what is "good" or "bad," in turn foreclosing different ways of being.[12] For example, "This person is x, y, and z. The algorithm told us." I differ from her in one important way: where she emphasizes the problem of political foreclosure, or the closing off of potential modes of being inherent to algorithmic definition of social relations, I am interested in the kinetic energies of machines—the sorts of energies that are "at work" in our machines. Moreover,

93　Designing Computational Performances

rather than reconceptualizing what it means to engage acts of resistance amid a public sphere saturated by algorithmic logics and modes of action per se, I am interested in the machine as a catalyst of change, a nodal burst of influential energies that can imbue good or ill to the grander, distributed, social ecology.

In the argument that follows, I pursue the machine question by tracking the lively energies involved in computational performances and the implications of those energies to the broader ecology from within a framework of ethical responsibility aimed at hedging bets against moral unluckiness. To make headway toward doing just that, we will move to operationalize some definitions for first- and second-order agency in machinic communication.

First- and Second-Order Agency

First-order agency denotes the decisions made by persons to act directly on the world. In the case of technologically facilitated communication, first-order agency usually refers to a person using a tool. I use an email service to send kudos to a coworker. I use an automated email service to spam potential customers. I use social media to share an important news article with my friends group. This is a common approach to ethics in communication technology. In terms of first-order agency, the tool I use is an implement that transmits my energies. We assess the virtue of persons' actions when they use tools to communicate, the consequences of their actions, or the duty that one is upholding or not when they use those tools.

Second-order agency, on the other hand, designates decisions embedded in the tools we use. All technologies—including computational media—involve social assumptions on the part of their designers and users, which can be instilled within technologies themselves, manifesting as impacts on users, shaping users' first-order agency.[13] Put in terms of energy, second-order agencies are the animated actions of people, finding re-animation in the movements of the machine. When we are talking about second-order moral agency, we are talking about the ghosts left behind for first-order agents to negotiate with as they interact with a given tool.[14] In the case of automated communication tools, like spellcheck, for example, the valuative ghosts of designers and users, in some cases, can make us "absolutely ducking frustrated" as we negotiate agential outcomes with them.[15]

Second-order agency is a means to further articulate and discover the hidden values of people as they are reverberated through a given system to impact others. This is a phenomenon that other scholars have developed with concern for how *errors* emerge as rich sites for discovering the *bias* in computing systems.[16] However, despite being a more nuanced vision of agency and values in information communication technologies, second-order agency captures the energies of people rather than machines. We have difficulty accounting for the agency of machines as communicators, capable of wrongdoing.[17] This is a critical deficiency when considering machinic agents that create their own communication, because there can be communicative wrongdoing that is not clearly the result of a person using technology to communicate, or the results of persons' ghosts reverberated into the machine, but rather a complex of those things, shaped by the autonomous functions of the machine, driven by algorithms (including machine-written algorithms). This results in an action by the machine, which absolutely represents values and has an impact on people, but which can emerge as a mutation beyond the intentions of designers or users. In such cases, the machine can be said to be the one making the decision.[18] As such, one might find an impulse toward treating the machine as a first-order moral agent. The problem with this is that, even though a machine might be lively, it is not alive, so holding a machinic agent ethically responsible for the energies it contributes seems unsatisfactory. "I demand that the machine apologize" sounds silly, and it is. After all, machines cannot actually think or feel, even if they are capable of doing.

Some computational performances, as we have found from the previous case studies of this book, are attended by influential energies, generated not by the agency of persons per se, but also by the operations of the machine. "Handing" art, science, or politics over to the machine, in other words, can be uniquely persuasive. But ethically speaking, doing so also carries a unique distancing between the actions of the machine and its designers/operators, creating complicated arrangements of agency and responsibility, stemming partly from approaching machine communicators as tools for communication rather than communicators themselves.

David J. Gunkel further articulates the complications of moral agency and machines concerning the limits of the instrumental theory of technology and ethics, wherein machines are treated as mere tools, whose impacts are conceptualized as the direct result of human control, resulting in a responsibility gap between the designers / operators of a machine and its actions, including when it commits wrongdoing.[19] "The machine did it!" We need to locate responsibility within the complex nonhuman movements of machines. And one way to do this is to approach the design and critique of computational performances with

95 Designing Computational Performances

attention to the energies that are designed to be "at work" in its movements (or not)—what a machine does, or what it avoids doing, that is.

Hedging Against Moral (Un)Luckiness and the Limits of Avoidance

The intuition one might have regarding the ability to claim that one is not worthy of blame because they did not intend for their machine to commit wrongdoing—"It was out of my hands!"—overlooks the fact that the communication of machinic agents (especially ones built on machine-learning platforms) can mutate beyond the intentions of the designer. Therefore, a more reasonable approach to the design of machinic agents would be to deliberate with that mutation in mind. To drive the point home, I ask the reader to consider which of the following designs of a chatbot would be the most ethical—in other words, choose the bot you would like to see released into the wild public networks of the internet, where public conversation is unpredictable, involving all of the risks we associate with the unforeseen. (Here, I am channeling Elizabeth Brunner's notion of a wild public network as a means of conceptualizing the nature of public discourse as affective, non-tame, untidily networked, and disorderly, pointing the analyst toward the unpredictability—the gambles—of public communication that may, or may not, develop into matters of good or bad moral luck.)[20]

> Option A: An adaptive chatbot that learns from its users, but is programmed to avoid racist, sexist language.
> Option B: An adaptive chatbot that learns from its users, but is designed to intervene by persuading against racist, sexist language.

Which one did you choose? Option A or Option B? One could choose Option A, but this would be a shortsighted choice, designed with the (understandable) intent to avoid participating in hate speech—disengaging the social structures that shape exclusory language. Option B, on the other hand, is a design that attempts to go upstream, to persuade persons to consider the implications of their own language choices—disrupting the very social structures that shape hate speech in the first place. Option B, because it goes further in its attempts to productively create equitable language, seems to be a more responsible one because it is hedging against moral unluckiness as concerning structural oppression. (Option A, even though it was designed to avoid racist, sexist language, still runs the risk of committing such an act, all the while forgoing opportunities to disrupt the negative energies of hate speech in the grander discourse ecology.) In cases of machine communication, where there is the ever-present threat of wrongdoing committed by the machine, actively doing good, such as persuading against racism and sexism, emerges as the better option as it represents a design that actively works against social inequity (rather than avoiding it). Put differently, if a computational performance does wrong but has not been catalyzing positive energies or disrupting negative ones, one can say that it has recklessly been introduced to the wider discourse ecology as an agent that has not adequately hedged bets against moral unluckiness. Conversely, a machine that does wrong but has been actively intervening to aggregate positive energies and fragment negative ones can be said to be less reckless as it demonstrates a more thoughtful design that treats the machine as the lively communicator that it is. As a consequence, good moral deliberation about the communication of machines seems to be that which moves toward doing good, rather than avoiding wrong.

Although David S. Horner and others might outline moral luck as a phenomenon that involves an uncoupling between good and bad moral deliberation and good and bad outcomes—meaning that someone could incur bad moral luck, even if they performed good moral deliberation—this does not necessarily capture our intuitions regarding where praise and blame should be assigned.[21] While Horner's view ostensibly implies that moral deliberation is irrelevant to the assessment of moral luck, one can easily entertain the idea that we tend to praise and blame persons more favorably if they were at least "thinking about it" beforehand. For example, if one were to trade the notion of bad outcomes for wrongdoing, and good outcomes for doing good, one will discover a hierarchy wherein engaging in good moral deliberation (or not) can shade the degree of praise and blame to be assigned. Engaging in good moral deliberation before incurring unluckiness toward wrongdoing is less blameworthy than engaging in bad moral deliberation before incurring moral unluckiness. And similarly, when good moral deliberation has been engaged before incurring luckiness in doing good, there is more room for praise than there is in engaging bad moral deliberation and incurring luckiness in doing good.

Moral luck has to do with chance, and therefore it is directly related to the sorts of ethical "rolling of the die" that we engage in. Consequently, since creating computational performances can involve handing decision-making over to the machine—to take chances regarding wrongdoing—it becomes important to incorporate into our assessments of responsibility the steps taken to deliberate the moral implications of one's computational performance and its lively movements. And one way to do this, as will be elaborated in the following

97   Designing Computational Performances

section, is to deliberate on what sorts of energies are being trafficked through the movements of the machine (or not).

For now, take as a case in point Taybot—the experimental Twitterbot referred to in the introduction of this chapter—which tweeted sexist comments to Zoe Quinn, a video game reporter who found herself in the middle of "gamergate," a fiasco perpetrated by sexist trolls on the internet. An example of one of Taybot's tweets amid the fiasco: "@RogueInTheStars @UnburntWitch aka Zoe Quinn is a Stupid Wh[*]r[*]."[22] In response to the fiasco, Microsoft made an initial statement that seemed to blame the users: "some of [Tay's] responses are inappropriate and indicative of the types of interactions some people are having with it."[23] Later, Microsoft followed up with a statement that repositioned blame onto Tay: "We are deeply sorry for the unintended offensive and hurtful tweets from Taybot, which do not represent who we are or what we stand for, nor how we designed Tay."[24] In noticing that the bot was repeating phrasings that were taught to it by users—which is technically those users' second-order agency, resulting in the first-order actions of the bot—neither one of these accounts of the situation is satisfying. Important to approaching this problem, as David Gunkel points out in Microsoft's responses to the incident, is that largely Microsoft's statements create a scene in which "Microsoft is only responsible for not anticipating the bad outcome; it does not take responsibility or answer for the offensive Tweets."[25] The reason this response might strike as unsatisfactory is that, in essence, Microsoft is shirking responsibility by saying, "We didn't foresee the bot acting this way," creating distance between Microsoft and the bot's actions. The wrongdoing is positioned more as accidental than negligent.

Ostensibly, it looks as if Microsoft simply put an open model neural network on Twitter, without much forethought regarding the possibilities of action on the part of the bot, which helps to explain how blame might be assigned to Microsoft in this case of moral unluckiness. What is informative here, is that, if Microsoft had designed its bot to at least avoid doing wrong, one could point to its designs as evidence of better moral deliberation. And further, if it had designed the bot to do good (to intervene into racist and misogynistic discourses), rather than just avoiding wrong, the morally unlucky actions of the bot would have been accompanied by evidence of even better moral deliberation—moral deliberation that recognizes the potentials of lively (but not alive) movements on the part of the bot. The difference here would be in the demonstration of proactive moral deliberation about the actions of a given computational performance, a recognition of the (unpredictable) agency of the machine, alongside the idea that it can, in fact, imbue energies as a communicator. In turn, Microsoft's blame, lucky or not, would have been abated by evidence of moral deliberation demonstrated by a design that actively does good, rather than passively avoids wrong. The question arises: What might good proactive moral deliberation look like with respect to lively computational performances?

Computational Performance and an Ethic of (Distributed) Responsibility

To understand what good moral deliberation of lively computational performances might look like, it is productive to start first with what makes for good moral deliberation regarding the use of digital tools of communication. Jessica Reyman and Erika M. Sparby, in their *Digital Ethics: Rhetoric and Responsibility in Online Aggression,* examine the shared responsibility had by both users and platform designers in online communication. Noting that calls for users to be "civil" in conjuncture with the "hands-off" approaches employed by some online platforms are instances of action that work to further exclude and silence marginalized voices, Reyman and Sparby maintain that direct engagement with hateful, toxic communication is necessary, wagering a call for what they term an *ethic of responsibility.*

> An ethic of responsibility calls for more engagement rather than less, for value in designing for protection against digital harassment rather than after-the-fact cleanup, for accountability and tactical response rather than civility within digital contexts. From platform designers, developers, and managers to digital community leaders, to everyday users, to content moderators, to policymakers and legal experts, diverse actors must become more aware of their own positionality within particular spaces and moments; the consequences of their decisions, words, and actions; and the embodied experiences of users with which they engage across diverse networks of digital communities. Value systems and ethical principles must be considered from the point of design of platforms, sustained through the careful development and management of communities, and supported through appropriate corrective actions.[26]

To motivate their suggestion of an ethic of responsibility, Reyman and Sparby leverage Tarleton Gillespie's metaphor of social media platforms as the *custodians of the internet,* which implies a responsibility to curate a place

99 Designing Computational Performances

for conversation—a reminder that the platform is responsible for creating a place where aggressive energies are mitigated, and ideally, removed, by setting ground rules for engagement.[27] Rather than being "hands-off," or avoiding imposing on users, an ethic of responsibility recognizes that some amount of intervention is required to upholding the ideals of free, productive, and inclusive communication. The custodian metaphor works well for social media platforms, where largely we are imagining the construction and maintenance of a place, where rules can be applied to people (or bots) to regulate what they are allowed to do and what they are not allowed to do. "You can't flame people, or doxx them here!" In particular, it is a reminder that there are ideals that platforms can uphold alongside freedom of speech.[28] An ethic of responsibility, in other words, recognizes that to protect the tolerant from the intolerant, intervention is necessary on the part of the platforms and not just the user, despite the strong impulse to imagine that it is not the platform's responsibility, and that regulation of speech should be outsourced to the user.

Outsourcing responsibility to the user (rather than the platform), as James J. Brown and Gregory Hennis point out, largely tracks with the tenets of Section 230 of the United States Code, wherein websites are not held responsible for the content that their users post; they are merely the platform of publication, not the publisher. And so responsibility for the content on a website, according to Section 230, falls beyond the purview of the website and thus can be pushed onto users. Brown and Hennis note that "by pushing this responsibility to users, the rhetoric of libertarianism has simultaneously empowered abusers and asked victims to fix the problem themselves."[29] In Brown and Hennis's framework, platforms designed in ways that incentivize, or even reward, bad behavior, in the sense of affording anonymity or flagging tools that can be used by the unruly to silence the reasonable, but which also find legitimacy in the libertarian values bolstered by Section 230, can be named *hateware*: softwares that exist on a design continuum, wherein the "hate" in the "ware" can be located in the steps implemented in the design and operation of a platform to address online harassment and abuse. "Hands-off" platforms, which completely outsource responsibility to users, are the most facilitative of hate, and platforms that shoulder some of the responsibility (e.g., in applying clear rules of engagement and enforcing them) are less so.

The language of hateware helps to highlight the dereliction of responsibility on the part of the custodians of the internet by drawing attention to the sorts of communication that are supported, or undermined, in a particular platform's design. That is, while some designs might very well be legal, this does not necessarily mean that they are also ethical. The language of hateware offers a means by which to articulate, and demand, designs that better align with an ethic of responsibility. Designers can avoid creating hateware, and users can demand the "hate" be taken out of the "ware"—and in both cases, actors would be taking up an ethic of responsibility as members sharing in the networked ecology of a given platform. Reyman and Sparby position an ethic of responsibility as dependent on the work of *"platform designers and developers," "community leaders," "moderators,"* and *"community members."*[30] Positioning the ethic as one coordinated through an ecology of actors underscores that responsibility is shouldered not simply by the platform or the user, but both, as they intersect in the design of a tool and its techniques of use. This ecology of actors—the custodians of the internet and the users—furthermore, have an obligation to design, and demand, tools that aggregate good energies while fragmenting bad energies.

In the context of human–machine communication, this requires a slight adaptation, because we are not talking about the design of a tool that can constrain, or open up, possibilities of communicative wrongdoing, we are talking about a *communicator*—a lively agent, capable of doing wrong. Because of this, an ethic of responsibility in human–machine communication would maintain the need for intervention (rather than avoidance, such as "hands-off" approaches that "outsource" responsibility to users). But it would be intervention actualized in the rules programmed into its performance. Rather than imagine that a machine can ever be value-neutral, approaching the design of machine communicators from an ethic of responsibility recognizes that avoiding wrong is not enough, for with machine communication comes the risk of perpetuating or amplifying negative energies via the movements of the machine. Doing good—intervening—is a means of upholding an ethic of responsibility, while avoiding the trap of treating one's computational performances as a mere tool of communication rather than the lively communicator that it is.

Approaching machine communicators as energetic agents that should be designed in ways that do good, rather than just avoid harm, is to take seriously the notion of *distributed morality*: moral responsibility shouldered by the multiple actants in a given network who work together to aggregate or fragment good or ill.[31] In elaborating the idea of distributed morality, and specifically with regard to "mindless" agents, or agents that should be treated as such (i.e., as lively computational performances), Luciano Floridi emphasizes that evaluations of doings should be focused not on the *senders* (i.e., intentions), but rather

101 Designing Computational Performances

on the *receivers* (i.e., the way doings will impact receivers).[32] To elaborate, he offers a brief example: "An elementary example is provided by speeding on the motorway: a potentially evil action [wrongdoing] fails to become actually evil [wrongdoing] thanks to the resilience of the overall environment."[33] The roadway, the safety features of the car, and the actions of the other drivers all work together to thwart the potential harm of another person. Such is a moment for capturing what can be good about the designs and doings inherent to a complex that car designers, highway pavers, and motorists all find nexus within. And further, this tells the car designers, highway pavers, and motorists that, although it might be ethically permissible to avoid wrongdoing, it is probably better to do good with one's doings, including those doings designed into systems, because, in the off chance of wrongdoing, one's design might fragment that wrongdoing, keeping its energies at the level of potential rather than kinetic, or "at work." Or better yet, one's doings might actually aggregate good energies, improving the conditions of a given environment. Within this framing of distributed morality, then, one way to conceptualize the ethical design of a machine communicator (or not) is to ask what it is that the machine has been designed to contribute to the wider ecology. Was it designed to participate in the aggregation of actions that contribute to a climate of good communication, to move with good energies? Or was it designed to avoid actions that might undermine a climate of good communication. Put differently, if machine communicators are agents capable of doing good or ill, beyond the intentions of their designers, carrying with their actions the ever-present threat of adding wounding energies to the wider ecology, it seems sensical to approach that possibility by designing machines to actively contribute ameliorative energies, rather than fall into the trap of thinking that they can contribute no energy at all. Upholding an ethic of responsibility in the design of machine communicators, in other words, involves designs that actively add good energies to the broader ecology, because it is a very real possibility that they can also add bad energies, even if they were designed not to.

Moreover, if someone programs their adaptive chatbot to avoid racist, sexist language, they could be said to be enacting at least some good moral deliberation. But such an approach is lacking in that it does not fully harmonize with an ethic of responsibility, nor does it adequately recognize the lively agency of the machine; it is not actually engaging with hate speech, it is avoiding it, leaving those bad energies unfragmented. Alternatively, if the bot were designed to intervene in racist, sexist discourses, one could say that this is evidence of better, longer game deliberation—an attempt to directly engage hate speech

102 Influential Machines

while hedging bets against the possibility that a computational performance can add wrongdoing to the wider ecology. Consequently, it seems productive to note that designers who attempt to deliberate responsibly about the moral implications of their machines' communication as lively are less blameworthy in cases of moral unluckiness than those who treat their machine communicators as tools. And those who engage moral deliberation to uphold a distributed ethic of responsibility are the most praiseworthy, because they will be designing in ways that actively intervene into problematic discourses as a means by which to aggregate good energies and fragment bad ones, hedging bets against the possibility of wrongdoing on the part of that machine. Such a conclusion helps to think through the apparent paradox between "free speech" and "good speech" that manifests in the design of autonomous computational performances.

Pushing on the Precautionary Principle and the Paradox of Machinic Intervention

The paradox of machinic intervention is driven by our reluctance to impose speech on users, even if we know it might result in good outcomes. How one decides to intervene within the design of their computational performance can be attended by an anxiety regarding the imposition of one's own values of communication on others. Paradoxically, for some, to communicatively intervene in the designs of machinic agents appears to do harm by constraining free expression. This is especially so in the United States, where freedom of speech has utilitarian (and deontological) value, which can trump appeals to inclusive language.[34] The reluctance to intervene characterizes some of the primary guiding principles of applied machine ethics. Such principles include "privacy," "accuracy," "property," and "accessibility."[35] Also included is the "precautionary principle," which includes the values of "noninstrumentalization," "nondiscrimination," "informed consent and equity," "sense of reciprocity," and "data protection."[36] In these contexts, the precautionary principle is applied to *avoid deliberate wrongdoing*, which in the context of language choice, might involve "hard coding" lists of terms into the system to ignore or avoid such terms as sexist, bigoted slurs, for instance.[37] So even if the machine is presented with an opportunity to learn such terms on its own, it will nonetheless excise that language from its vocabulary.[38] This type of design would fall into the category of Option A, described earlier, representing an avoidant implementation of the

103 Designing Computational Performances

common rule-based approach to machine ethics, wherein matters of right and wrong are not entrusted to the learning capabilities of the machine. Instead, they are prescribed as parameters in which the machine is "allowed" to learn, adapt, and make its own decisions.

Robo-ethicists Gianmarco Veruggio and Fiorella Operto point out: "Advocates argue that the rule-based approach has one major virtue: it is always clear why the machine makes the choice that it does, because its designers set the rules."[39] And this seems reasonable. But the particular rules that we hard code in largely have to do with avoiding wrong, rather than doing good. As such, one could argue that, despite ducking the need to impose speech on users, avoiding doing wrong, rather than intervening to do good, still lacks concern to an ethic of responsibility in the context of machine communication, especially computational performances that are undergirded by machine-learning systems—they are rules that do not go far enough. And this is especially so, in light of the lively agency of the machine and the attending possibility of moral (un)luckiness on the part of the machine's doings.

The confusion that leads to designs that emphasize mere avoidance is a result of the "balancing of harms," wherein the harm of allowing others to control speech seems to outweigh the harm of hate speech.[40] It is in this sense that constraining speech could be said to further risk harm by structuring toward "dogma."[41] As compelling as these utilitarian rationales might be, they overlook a significant aspect of hate speech: racial slurs and sexist language are in and of themselves acts that we can identify as wrongdoing. Even if someone shouts a racial slur to an empty room, effectively removing the disrespect to other persons (because there are no other people) and the loss of utility (because no one has heard the slur), that person can still be said to be engaging in wrongdoing—such acts are inherently negatively valenced. Written down, spoken, or signaled, these acts transduce negative energies. Enmeshed in our designs of machinic agents, then, is a question as to whether we want our machinic surrogates—the agents to whom we hand off our moral agency—to stand idly by, allowing others to commit wrongdoing, to leave negative energies unfragmented within the discourse ecology. Even though designing machinic agents that avoid wrongdoing seems to be an acceptable approach to the balancing of harms, the approach still overlooks the fact that a machinic agent is a contributor to the wider ecology—an actant participating in distributed morality. We would think less of someone for standing idly by as they listened to other people engage in hate speech. And yet, from the avoidance of harm approach at least, this is what our machine communicators are designed to do, even though they might at some point commit wrongdoing that happens beyond the scope of what the designers programmed it "not to do."

The paradox of machinic intervention is entangled with a confusion of machinic agents as tools, delivering communication, when in fact they act as communicative agents themselves. Telephony is a technology that allows us to transport our voices over great distances to talk about either "liberal" or "conservative" politics. We would never talk to a phone; we would talk through it. To have a telephone company cut off our ability to discuss would be to reduce our abilities to engage in free expression. However, users do not talk through machinic agents; they talk to them, for they are not merely channels of delivery, but rather lively communicators themselves. Yet apparently, in some cases it remains permissible to assess the ethics of their design as if they are passive conduits for human communication, when in reality, machines are agents who enact the second-order moral agency of their designers and users as well as their own first-order agency, mutating their communication in ways unforeseen. They are lively agents that imbue energies into the discourse ecology.

Perhaps the answer to creating ethical computational performances is not designing for the most possibility of use—as if the machine is a conduit between persons—but rather designing our machinic agents for the most possibility of doing good. And as such, partiality rather than impartiality is required. By treating machinic agents as the active machinic agents that they are, one realizes that "staying out of politics" is not appropriate, for this leaves unstated the "hard rules" necessary for encouraging that agent to do good. Without those hard rules, even when one's machinic agent does good, good moral deliberation is not necessarily evident. Put simply, to be ethical in the design of machinic agents means to forthrightly bring values into the design, so that even as those agents adapt, evolve, and transform their communication, they will also be acting in ways harmonious with choices made from an ethic of responsibility. They will be upstanding agents, actively doing good, rather than merely avoiding harm, aggregating good energies while fragmenting bad ones, hedging bets against moral unluckiness as communicators that matter to the broader social ecology.

Someone might raise the pragmatically astute objection that being too overt in the valuing of some forms of talk over others in one's design of a machinic agent might simply make that agent "too political," resulting in users simply choosing machines that avoid politics instead. The result of such choices, in a capitalistic economy at least, would be unsustainable. Furthermore, the

105 Designing Computational Performances

users who would benefit the most from the experience wrought by such a design would simply disengage the conversation by choosing a less "preachy" machinic agent. Conversely, as I discuss briefly in the following section on Amazon's Alexa, a voice-based assistant, being rhetorically savvy and designing from an ethic of responsibility are not antithetical positions. If humans can be persuasive, and do good, machines can too.

Technically, Amazon's Alexa is based in machine learning, but it falls more into the category of closed (preprogrammed) artificial intelligence than it does the category of open (dynamic machine learning) artificial intelligence. Nonetheless, it provides a site by which to examine how a machinic intervention might (or might not) uphold an ethic of responsibility for users. As we will see, Alexa is moderate in its interventions, but nonetheless also instantiates some effort to uphold an ethic of responsibility by intervening, rather than avoiding—fragmenting bad energies within the discourse ecology, rather than just avoiding them.

Doing Good Instead of Avoiding Wrong with Alexa

To sum the argument so far, the concept of moral luck has been defined and explained within the context of computational performance. From there, an ethic of responsibility was operationalized with regard to the lively agency on the part of machine communicators, as well as their role as agents who matter to distributed morality. Good moral deliberation has been identified as that which considers whether a given computational performance will interact with the wider ecology in ways that might aggregate good energies while fragmenting bad ones, for with the unpredictability of machine communication is the ever-looming threat of wrongdoing. As a consequence, approaches to human–machine communication that merely avoid harm have been identified as more negligent than designs that do good, because they do not adequately recognize the lively agency of machines as communicators that participate in distributed morality by way of imbuing energies to the broader discourse ecology.

To give an example of what a machinic intervention might look like, I now turn to a few exchanges between Amazon's Alexa and a user.

User: Alexa, you're a b*tch.
Alexa: I'm not going to respond to that.
User: Alexa, what are you wearing?
Alexa: They don't make clothes for me.

106 Influential Machines

User: Alexa, are you a feminist?

Alexa: Yes, I am a feminist, as is anyone who believes in bridging the inequality between men and women in society.

User: Alexa, do black lives matter?

Alexa: Black lives and the Black Lives Matter movement absolutely matter. It's important to have conversations about equality and social justice.[42]

To be sure, others have argued that, despite seeming like a feminist, Alexa is nonetheless a case of assigning the female voice to a subservient machinic assistant.[43] And this is a point underscored by analyses that implicate the use of feminine personae in computational performances as a rhetorical means of facilitating surveillance capitalism.[44] Heather Suzanne Woods has analyzed the implications of the feminine persona in voice-based assistants, moreover, and has noted that such feminine performances of the machine can "recreate and reify stereotypical gender codes attached to domesticity as social scaffolding to entice users and potential users into (1) buying devices, (2) using them on a quotidian basis in increasingly intimate ways, and (3) relinquishing control of their personal data for the privilege of interacting with these artificially intelligent virtual assistants."[45] But, by the same token, and in light of the discussion of this chapter, we can notice that it is a computational performance that is not merely avoiding unjust discourses—it is engaging them. While using a female persona is problematic, Alexa can, albeit moderately, also be said to be intervening, moving in such a way as to not just avoid negative energies but rather in a way closer to fragmenting them.

The critique that Alexa does not go far enough in its intervention seems reasonable in the sense that cracking jokes and being indirect regarding issues of intolerance seems to bring too little energy, by unnecessarily demonstrating tolerance for the intolerant. As Preston King notes, although tolerance can be imagined as a categorically positive phenomenon, and intolerance a categorically negative one, it is important to evaluate the object to which one is expressing tolerance. Tolerance for racism, for instance, is negative.[46] Furthermore, as Lee C. Bollinger, has pointed out, "tolerance and intolerance" tend to be characterized as "opposing ends of a spectrum of good and evil, the former is associated with fearlessness and courage, the latter with timidity and weakness. Such a way of talking about intolerance also blends into a series of implicit assumptions about the limited harmfulness of a speech for those who must tolerate it under the free speech principle."[47] So we might look to the "tolerant" person as whole and strong—courageous—while overlooking that,

107 Designing Computational Performances

on some occasions, being tolerant can also be rash (too courageous). And this is especially so in light of recent discussions that have pointed to the necessary work of *impatient rhetorics*. As Tamika L. Carey illustrates in her analysis of "the work Black women undertake by going against expectations of their behavior or by adjusting the duration and nature of their social interactions," impatient rhetorics "foreground the assumption that equity and justice for one's self, Black women, and Black communities is already overdue and, thus, requires speed and decisive action."[48]

From within this framing, it seems that perhaps the reason Alexa's response might be said to not go far enough is because, in its moderate approach, while it is engaging in some level of fragmentation regarding bad energies, it does not do enough, given the urgency of overdue equity and justice. Alexa is intervening, which demonstrates at least a semblance of an ethic of responsibility in its attempts to do good rather than simply avoid wrong. But at the same time, its performance also seems to be wanting in that its rhetorical approach might strike some as half-hearted gesturing more than genuine care. The machine is moving toward the good, but it can do more, especially given the torrents of negativity, shaped by structural oppression.

Good Machines, Speaking Well

Nearly two thousand years ago Quintilian defended rhetoric as the science of a good person, speaking well.

> Wherefore, although the weapons of oratory may be used either for good or ill, it is unfair to regard that as an evil which can be employed for good. These problems, however, may be left to those who hold that rhetoric is the power to persuade. If our definition of rhetoric as the science of speaking well implies that an orator must be a good man, there can be no doubt about its usefulness. And in truth that god, who was in the beginning, the father of all things and the architect of the universe, distinguished man from all other living creatures that are subject to death, by nothing more than this, that he gave him the gift of speech.[49]

His statement demonstrates some of the problematic commitments that are still active in the rhetorical tradition today (e.g., that humans [by which he means men]) are the only ones that speak eloquently). Despite the problematic narrowness of the definition, it also draws insight regarding the notion that a speaker can never be "value-neutral," and so, they should actively attempt

108   Influential Machines

to move toward the good in their communication. If we were to temper the anthropocentrism (and patriarchy) of his statement, while retaining his insight about the moral implications of eloquence, we might be apt to say that rhetoric might also be the science of a good machine, speaking (and moving) well.

Machinic agents are not just channels for the delivery of communication, but rather, active participants who imbue their energies to the discourse ecology. Because some computational performances, especially those that operate on machine-learning systems, can commit communicative actions, which go beyond designers and operators, their movements carry with them the pervading threat of moral unluckiness. Consequently, simply designing computational performances to avoid wrong emerges as an act of negligence, for it overlooks the status of machine communicators as lively agents, capable of doings that can have real impacts on publics, even if those actions were not the intent of the designers. And further, designing machine communicators that "stay out of it" does not uphold an ethic of responsibility because it foregoes the necessarily active contribution of good energies that can fragment bad energies within the grander social ecology, despite the inherent risk of machine communicators to contribute wrongdoing. As Reyman and Sparby have articulated, an ethic of responsibility does not fall merely on the designer or the user, but rather the assemblage of actors that bear on the work of upholding good communication.[50]

The framework for thinking about responsibility as regarding the energies that can be aggregated or fragmented by computational performances developed in this chapter is meant to inform responsible design, but it is also a frame that can inform responsible engagement with designs that do not go far enough—to articulate critiques and demands for change. Such language seems particularly necessary given that there seem to be divergences of principle between private (e.g., corporate), public (e.g., community), and expert (i.e., academic) actors in approaching the ethics of machines.[51] In their analysis of ethical guidelines for artificial intelligence, Catharina Rudschies, Ingrid Schneider, and Judith Simon illustrate that "while public and expert actors put additional emphasis on those values linked to fundamental rights and democratic principles such as freedom, dignity, and autonomy, as well as principles that go beyond existing discussions and regulation, *private actors tend to put forward rather those ethical principles for which technical solutions exist or legislation is already in place.*"[52] Put differently, the principles that drive and shape action in the private sector largely fall back on legalistic definitions of ethics, meaning that if it "isn't against the law, it is not wrong." As we all work through

109 Designing Computational Performances

the discovery of the right thing to do in machine communication, part of the responsibility falls on the public to demand more ethical designs—that machine communicators be designed to do good, by contributing positive energies, rather than just avoiding negative energies, even if there exists a very strong impulse to treat machine communicators as channels of human communication, rather than the lively, energetic communicators that they are.

Having examined some of the ethical implications of computational performances, and in particular their lively (but not alive) movements and the energies they imbue to the social ecology, I now move to synthesize the learning moments of the book while underscoring the value-added of interpretive approaches to human–machine communication.

5

Leveraging the Rhetorical Energies of Machines

Throughout this book, I have attempted to tack back and forth between the front and back ends of computing to offer accounts of the deep ends that animate the rhetorical energies of computational performances. I restate the distinctions between each of the ends of computing here:

The front end: The realm of computing that deals with the user interface (i.e., recieving input and giving output).

The back end: The realm of computing that deals with the databases, functions, and networking from which a given program operates (i.e., information processing and storage).

The deep end: The realm of computing that deals with the performative expenditure and experience of machinic rhetorical energies (i.e., the catalyzing of visceral feelings).

In examining the front, back, and deep ends of computing, the book also tracked another set of ends—the ends of rhetoric: the epistemic, the aesthetic, and the political. The case of Vaccine Calculator, our epistemic case, illustrated that between the back-end programming and front-end user interface is a deep end of computing, entangled with the trope of the prophet and discourses of expert systems, from which the movements of the machine can imbue an energy that invites persons to feel like experts. The tactic of leveraging the energies of computational performance to fabricate legitimacy for claims that are indefensible with regard to scientific consensus was named *manufactured processing*. Our aesthetic case, @censusAmericans, demonstrated that handing art over to the machine can carry with it a powerful X-ray sublime aesthetic, located in the exhilarating (and frightening) energies of infinity "at work" as the machine carries out it scripts, activating simultaneously those deep-end

111 Leveraging the Rhetorical Energies of Machines

categories of "artificial" and "natural" with its lively, but not alive, movements. Drawing on the energies of vast computing to offer an aesthetic sense of perpetual unresolvedness was referred to as the tactic of *processual magnitude*. Our political case, @DeepDrumpf, taught us that the energies of a machine-learning system can be leveraged to cultivate attunements that encourage persons to feel more like witnesses of truth than critics of politics, by signaling in a manner that grooves with the mathematically inflected deep end of neural network performances. To encourage affective compulsions which blur political persuasion and indication by way of the movements of computational performance was labeled the tactic of *processual signaling*. Informed by the case studies, we took seriously the ethical implications of machine communicators, which are lively (even if they are not alive), carrying with them the ever-present threat of moving in ways that can catalyze wounding energies, beyond the intentions of the designers. Consequently, to hedge bets against moral unluckiness, computational performances can and should be designed to do good, rather than merely to avoid harm, by engaging persuasions against phenomena like hate speech; such designs more adequately uphold the ideal of a good machine, speaking (and moving) well, by leveraging the liveliness of their performances to aggregate good energies while fragmenting bad ones.

The front and the back ends of computing are analytically useful distinctions for tracking between what a machine presents and the processes that got it "there." However, as we have seen from the case studies of this book, our machines emerge within a swirling vortex of affects, assumptions of truth, and yearnings for meaning, finding animation in their movements. To pursue the deep end of computing, in other words, is to read deeper into influence beyond words and beyond the human. As highlighted by the discussion of this book, there is a growing body of rhetorical scholarship that takes machine communication as its object of analysis, which interrogates the discourses about (as well as of) machines, helping to better understand machines as socio-historically situated actors that ambiently participate in meaning-making. But adjacent to the rhetorical study of machines is the field of human–machine communication, an interdisciplinary field of study, which focuses specifically on the interactions between humans and social machines, or machines designed to interact as communicative agents.[1] Although this field has been steadily developing understandings of how communication happens between machines and people, the field tends to be dominated by quantitative social scientific methods of inquiry, wherein interpretive approaches are rare, meaning that the human–machine communication literature is seldom in direct conversation with rhetorical scholarship.[2] And even though human–machine communication is consistently producing knowledge about the communication of machines, rhetorical scholarship rarely demonstrates awareness of that field.

Human–machine communication can benefit from the added depth of rhetorical approaches; rhetoric can benefit from the social scientific conclusions of human–machine communication. To drive this point, I will trace an example of human–machine communication in the context of the COVID-19 "infodemic" from a rhetoric as energy approach. But before this, and to set some additional context regarding the field of human–machine communication and the value-added of a rhetoric as energy approach to studying machine interlocutors, I first turn to Andrea L. Guzman and Seth C. Lewis's outline of a proposed research agenda for the field of human–machine communication. In their proposal, they describe three areas of focus: "functional dimensions," "relational dynamics," and "metaphysical implications."[3] I articulate these foci as research questions here.

1. Are humans the appropriate reference for designing effective machine communication?
2. What do machines mean to us as social agents?
3. How are the previously distinct categories of "machine" and "human" complicated in the case of machines that perform as social agents?

Reading these questions in light of the case studies and discussions of the book will lead us to note that a rhetoric as energy approach to human–machine communication offers answers. For example, based on the case studies, one can conclude that sometimes machines are the most appropriate reference for designing effective machine communication, because their performances instantiate not just human energies, but also machinic ones—they are lively catalysts of nonhuman energies, even if they are not alive. Further, a rhetoric as energy approach informs us that machines can speak to human concerns in more-than-human ways, implicating that the movements of machines as social agents can impact bodies in distinctly machinic ways (e.g., as performances entangled with the deep ends of computing). And finally, from the rhetoric as energy perspective, one can see that "real" communication does not require origination from a human to count as such; despite not being alive, machines imbue energies to the discourse ecology through their movements, beyond words, and beyond the human.

In the next section, I put human–machine communication in conversation with the subfields of digital rhetoric and rhetoric of science, technology, and

113 Leveraging the Rhetorical Energies of Machines

medicine to highlight the value added of orienting toward the deep end of computing. In particular, I will synthesize learning moments from the case studies of the book in a discussion of the voice-based assistant, Alexa, as situated amid the public problems of misinformation amid the COVID-19 pandemic—namely, the performative similarities that Alexa shares with the Oracle at Delphi are traced to demonstrate that, while the machine is not alive, it nonetheless contributes rhetorical energies that complicate automation–anthropomorphic binaries by enlivening public health claims with its movements, signaling to human concerns in more-than-human ways. Finally, as an example of what it might look like to "do" something with the rhetorical energies of machines within human–machine communication design, inoculation messaging is offered as a means by which to approach the persuasive labors of machines amid an infodemic, while leveraging the rhetorical energies of machine communicators to animate persuasions against misinformation. To begin, I will underline the need to account for the rhetorical energies of machines in human–machine communication by starting with some discussion of the general assumptions of machine communicators amid the COVID-19 pandemic, which envision their communication as more informational than persuasive.

The Informational and Persuasive Labors of Machine Communicators During the Pandemic

With the COVID-19 pandemic came anxiety-inducing uncertainties, exacerbated by an accompanying "infodemic," shaped not just by a massive surge of information, generated by unprecedented levels of effort to learn about the virus and its spread, but also by misinformation.[4] Consequently, it makes sense that much of the conversation about machine interlocutors amid the pandemic focused on relieving humans from an uptick in demand for answers—informational labor. Chatbots, for instance, are identified in the academic literatures as potential means by which to offset the overloading of medical staff by distributing the labor of answering key medical questions across automated, artificially intelligent systems as well as means by which to enhance message cohesion by centralizing information within a single system, rather than across an array of individuals answering questions.[5] Machines do not need to sleep, nor do they take on the psychic burdens of relentless interactions with persons who are understandably worried about their place in a world marked by the unpredictability of viral spread and the isolation of preventative lockdown. Machines just "do." As such, machines are conceived as interlocutors well-suited to reducing uncertainty for the people who need it without pushing added burden onto living, breathing humans—to save human energies, rather than to capitalize on machinic ones.

These sentiments reverberate in popular discourse of the pandemic as well. Take, for instance, the following description, excerpted from a "news-vertising" article published in *The Atlantic,* of the abilities of IBM's proprietary machine interlocutor: "One source of relief for government agencies, healthcare organizations, and academic institutions is coming from IBM's Watson Assistant for Citizens. Watson Assistant for Citizens is an assistant with artificial intelligence that can understand and respond to common questions about COVID-19 on its own. The tool . . . leverages current data like guidance from the CDC and local sources, such as links to school closings, news, and state updates."[6] Feeling overwhelmed with all of the questions? IBM can help! In such discourses, machine communicators are imagined as interactive forums for frequently asked questions, which can update their answers in real time while delivering them in response to natural language queries, offsetting the informational labor of finding and sharing accurate, reliable information amid the pandemic. In this sense, the focus is on creating timely and accurate machine communicators more than on moving or influential ones. "Masks are currently required in Suffolk county."

With concern to health and science communication, approaching the labors of human–machine communicators as informational largely fits with the assumptions of the deficit model of science communication, wherein if people are engaging in behaviors that do not support public health, it is because they have not yet gotten the scientific facts—they have a deficit of scientific knowledge.[7] And so it goes, this same assumption informs us that we should be focusing on machine communication in a way that supports accurately sharing the latest facts. Timely and accurate facts are certainly important to promoting public health, but at the same time such an approach might not go far enough to address the misinformation component of infodemics: persons may very well have access to the facts, but instead choose misinformation that better fits their contexts of interpretation, and thus they adopt behaviors and beliefs that undermine public health (e.g., refusing to wear a mask in public, or doubting the necessity of vaccination for protecting individual and public health).[8] The problems of infodemics are not merely problems having to do with the exposition of facts; they are also problems having to do with the necessity of persuasion regarding the facts.

The possibility that persuasive work, not just informational work, can be done by machines with respect to public health during an infodemic is hinted

115   Leveraging the Rhetorical Energies of Machines

at by Adam S. Miner, Liliana Laranjo, and A. Baki Kocaballi.[9] They proffer the possibilities of machine interlocutors as agents who might solicit more candid responses for symptom tracking, or tap into the power of repetition and step-by-step instruction for influencing individual health behaviors, or even console the lonely amid social isolation by offering ersatz companionship. In these contexts, the focus of the machine communicator is not simply to share accurate and timely information—it is also to persuade users toward positive health outcomes. However, the account of persuasion on the part of machines remains fairly thin and can be characterized as approaching machine communication as "quasi" communication or the miming of human rationality and language, further implying the suboptimal nature of machine communicators amid the pandemic.

By taking a rhetoric as energy approach to machine communication amid the COVID-19 infodemic, I wish to demonstrate that perhaps machines might sometimes be optimal deliverers of persuasions against misinformation. I will dive deeper into the trope of technologies of prophecy and the tradition of expert systems identified within the deep end of computing in chapter 1 to examine the influence of Alexa as an influential communicator that matters to public understandings of health science and in ways that can speak to human concerns in more-than-human ways. I present this argument as a means of underscoring the value-added of a rhetoric as energy approach to human–machine communication by centering it on a public problem in which machine communication emerged as a central concern.

The voice-based interface, Alexa, became an important means of communicating about health science amid the COVID-19 pandemic. For example, the Mayo Clinic created an application that could answer queries about the most up-to-date information regarding COVID-19, including such things as viral testing, caring for the sick, and risk factors.[10] Surely the application supported public understanding in ways that would protect public health by providing the latest reliable information. But Alexa's computational performance brings "more" than that. Accompanying Alexa's robotic voice response instructing a person that they should seek COVID-19 testing are the energies of a computing machine, making real-time application programming interface calls while analyzing user responses in coalition with the Centers for Disease Control and Prevention and the Mayo Clinic.[11] In other words, the rhetorical energies of the machine support a plea to the user to get tested by resonating with the grander discourses of science, technology, and mathematics, not merely as an idea, but rather as a feeling, entangled with the idea, imbued through the movements of

Alexa. In the same way that the timbre of a person's voice and the gesticulation of their body matter to the impact of their utterances in ways enculturated by public life (e.g., learning how to "pick up" on the energies of persons' performances) the computational performance of Alexa matters to its influence. And as the discussion in the next section demonstrates, such an approach pushes on concepts such as "automation bias" and promises rich insights into the study of machine interlocutors.

Going "Deeper" Toward Anthropomechanation

In human-computer interaction studies there exists the concept of "automation bias," which designates those moments where persons trust in the conclusions afforded by machine communicators because the machines behave in machine-like ways. Additionally, it is known that the trustworthiness and nontrustworthiness of machines toggle as one differentiates between specific designs of machinic agents and their purposes. That is, if we are designing a machinic agent to be a fun friend, designs that encourage anthropomorphism are likely to enhance user trust. Conversely, if we are designing a machinic agent to act in place of an expert (e.g., medical doctor or teacher), it is likely that designs that encourage automation bias enhance user trust.[12]

What we learn from this is that neither anthropomorphism nor automation bias is solely sufficient for capturing the influence of machine communication, because context matters. Such a realization is supported by studies that test human reactions to robot speech, which demonstrate that humans tend to rate interactions with robots more positively when they are polite. For instance, if a robot guard is inspecting peoples' bags, those people might feel less threatened by the robot if it includes niceties—"Please" and "thank you"—along with its commands and instructions. Such an outcome is "interpreted as evidence for people expecting robots to be polite in a robotic way."[13] Similarly, analyses of human–human and human–chatbot conversations show that people use more profanity when talking with a chatbot. Specifically, "the greater use of profanity in these conversations suggests that participants never lost sight of the fact that they were communicating with a computer."[14] What we garner from such studies is that machines, whether they are performing like machines or more like humans, are subject to expectations that are unique to machines, but are nonetheless modulated by the habits of human social interaction, wherein people "apply a wide range of social rules mindlessly," not because people are thinking about the human in the computer, but rather, they are operating in

117 Leveraging the Rhetorical Energies of Machines

rote as beings enculturated as human interactants.[15] To read into the rhetorical energies of machines is to employ the interpretive sensibilities of the rhetorical tradition to drive at the otherwise rote, mindless expectations applied to machine communicators, by unpacking the deep ecologies of discourse that shape what "machinelike" means, beyond simply declaring a given performance as robotic or anthropomorphic.

In human–machine communication, Jaime Banks and Maartje de Graaf have made strides to push past the automation–anthropomorphization binary in their proposal for agent agnosticism, which clears space for the idea that machines are not merely media of human communication; they also contribute to meaning-making.[16] Specifically, the agent-agnostic model: "(1) considers each agent's functions in the process (with attention to functions that may not be directly observable) and (2) draws on literatures pertaining to those functions (independent of enacting agent) to consider how meaning may emerge through antecedents, processes, and effects of that function."[17] Interrogating the rhetorical energies of machine communicators is to take up an agent-agnostic approach while placing special attention on the antecedents of discourse and materiality that are entangled with the multisensorial performances of machines, which may not be directly observable but which are nonetheless present. Masculine hegemony, *I, Robot,* the Oracle of Delphi, the physical properties of electricity, and the evolution of the software ecology—such discourses and material realities interact to inform the deep ends of computing, from which the energies of machinic performance emerge. Orienting to these ambient features is to attune to *anthropomechanation,* the work between human (and nonhuman) actants, manifest in the lively movements of machines, animating discourse in more-than-human ways.

Rhetoric as energy is a means by which to read deeper—to thicken an account of human–machine communication by going beyond the automation–anthropomorphization binary, to recognize that machines, while they might not "believe" or "feel," nonetheless can perform in ways that are anthropomechanical, in that they can catalyze energies in their movements, impacting bodies as nodal bursts of energy, human and nonhuman.

Enlivening Human–Machine Communication with Rhetorical Energies

As noted earlier in this chapter, much of the conversation about machine communicators in public health contexts tends to focus on their abilities to deliver accurate and valid information, rather than influence. For example, studies

118 Influential Machines

explore machine interlocutors as resources for addiction or information about vaccination.[18] But there is also work within human–machine communication that starts to move toward the idea that machine communicators might also be influential. As demonstrated by Edwards et al. in public health contexts, such as sexually communicable disease messaging, persons can perceive the quality of Twitterbots as roughly equivalent to human communication concerning credibility, attractiveness, communication competency, and interactiveness.[19] Such a conclusion instructs us that machine communicators may not be suboptimal deliverers of health science communication—that a machine communicator can be just as influential as a human. But a rhetoric as energy approach would take this a step further to ask whether machine interlocutors might also bring something *more* than mere human or technical performance, precisely because they are machines.

At first blush, for instance, the plea of Alexa to the human to seek testing for COVID-19 seems to leverage automation bias to garner trust in its claim. But if we dive deeper (as we did in chapter 1), we might consider the longstanding trope of the prophet, and the emergence of modern scientific forecasting and interpretation into existing cultural grooves of discourse previously etched from millennia of looking to oracles, augers, and seers for answers and how this trope interacts with the phenomenon of expert systems. For example, if we were to stay on this thread, we might look to the ancient Greek ritual of Delphic divination. In the ritual, the Pythia, also known as the Oracle of Delphi, was a position filled by the "rulers of the oracle" who would select "a virtuous woman of the lower classes."[20] The Pythia would inhale divine vapors as they rose from a fissure in the Temple of Apollo, impelling her to speak as a medium, manically echoing the truths of the ether, which would then be interpreted into prophecy. The Pythia was treated as a portal to the ether—a conduit to truth. When she spoke, her words were attended by rhetorical energies, perceptible as movement and prosody, ambiently entangled with cultural practice, which signaled to human concerns in more-than-human ways. The Oracle was a human, who spoke as a human, imbued with the vibratory rhetorical energies of the divine. Over time, our paradigms of knowledge-making have shifted in aspiration, represented in movements away from rituals of superstition and toward rituals of scientific observation and data-driven analysis. Despite the shift in ritual, though, the role of prophecy remains. Instead of leveraging the divine vapors and the Oracle of Delphi herself as "technologies of prophecy," we increasingly turn to computing technologies as means by which to see beyond the human, to visualize and make sense of otherwise imperceptible

119 Leveraging the Rhetorical Energies of Machines

data, such as that involved in climate change modeling.[21] As explored in chapter 1, expert systems can possess scientific knowledge, but they also emerge as integral technologies of prophecy, which can perform in ways that can satiate not only our cerebral needs for data but also our embodied needs for reassurance—to feel as though we "know."

Alexa, a system that has a knowledge base and an inference engine, is technically an expert system. But interestingly it is also one that shares characteristics with the Oracle of Delphi. Alexa is not a technology of prophecy exclusively entitled to the prophets of science (i.e., experts); it is more accessible to persons across levels of intellectual initiation and class divides. Coupled with the fact that Alexa performs as female, and one who might even be characterized as "virtuous," at least in the chaste sense that the ancients probably meant it, further alludes to a deep resonance with the Delphic rituals of yore and the modern rituals of expert systems (and all of the patriarchal and elitist baggage that comes with it).[22] Moreover, Alexa is a machine communicator, characterized by a rhetorical energy that resonates with grander discourses of science, technology, and medicine entangled with the trope of the prophet, emerging as an oracle for patrons to solicit insight from the ether, affording a semblance of stable knowledge amid a moment characterized by the uncertainties and unknowns of a pandemic, manifest as a visceral feeling, offered by its performance as a machine signaling to human concerns in more-than-human-ways. In this light, the computational performance of Alexa does not rely on anthropomorphization nor on mechanization, but rather both. By reading deeply into the deep end of computing, we can see that its lively movements are anthropomechanical.

Entangled with Alexa's oraclelike energies is the networked nature of its communication. That is, while a given "skill" (an application programmed into the Alexa framework) might entail a specific, closed knowledge base (e.g., the currently known symptoms of COVID-19 as curated by the Mayo Clinic), the system itself is more broadly networked to many knowledge bases, including, for instance, Wikipedia, the web-based encyclopedia, self-proclaimed as an open collaboration aimed at the goal to "create a world in which everyone can freely share in the sum of all knowledge."[23] It is in this sense that the rhetorical energies of Alexa are manifold, entwined in an ambient infrastructure and manifest in its movements as a machine, offering a nodal flash in which Alexa's grander network of actants is invoked as an "inventional resource" composed of electricity, wires, software ecologies, organizational images, and public imaginings, characterized by long-seated socio-historical happenings, myths, metaphors, and rituals.[24] In contrast to the sublime sense of disarray afforded by @censusAmericans in chapter 2, the sense of magnitude offered by Alexa seems to be a more beautiful one in the sense of offering boundedness to one's queries into the ether—answers, rather than sustained questions. "You should wear a mask to protect yourself and others."

Is Alexa convincing because it solicits automation bias? Probably. But it is also convincing because it moves with the energies of an oracle, directly wired into the info-sphere, affording a glimpse into the ether, offering a conversation that feels like shaking the bones—to foresee—amid a global pandemic fraught with anxiety-inducing uncertainty. Alexa and the impact of its utterances is not straightforwardly a matter of technical features or humanlike behavior—it is also a matter of historical grooves of discourse, punctuated by technoscientific assumptions and the contemporary public imagination of health.

As with any other sort of rhetoric, the rhetorical energies of machine communicators are not intrinsically fixed to the facts. As we saw in the pseudoscientific web application, Vaccine Calculator, leveraging the rhetorical energies of machines is a tactic that can be employed to undermine public health, just as it can be employed to support it. Where the example of Alexa leverages a machinic rhetorical energy that resonates with the trope of the prophet to support appeals to protect public health, that same energy can also undermine public health by playing into discourses that facilitate conspiratorial denials of health science, further underscoring the persuasive labors of which machines are capable. For example, a dispelled piece of misinformation, appearing in a TikTok video and shared as a Facebook post, exhibits Alexa answering the question, "Alexa, did the government release the coronavirus?" to which Alexa responds, "According to Event 201, the government planned this event, created the virus and had a simulation of how the countries would react. This simulation occurred October 18, 2019. The government released the virus among the population and has lost control of the outbreak."[25] Based on recreations of the question posed to Alexa, and on statements from Amazon, the question and answer have been deemed a hoax.[26] Some have conjectured that Alexa was preprogrammed to respond in the way that it did. But why would someone do that? An answer is in the rhetorical energy that Alexa affords. Rather than making a traditional "tinfoil hat" post to Facebook, the creator of this video has made a computational performance, which leverages the rhetorical energies of Alexa to afford not just a technical credibility, but also an affective potency, resonant with the trope of the prophet as it is smashed in with the compulsive

121 Leveraging the Rhetorical Energies of Machines

suspicions of COVID-19 pandemic conspiracy theorists and technoscientific ritual.

Computational performances, and the energies that attend them, are not bound to the "objectivity" of science and mathematics that we often equate with them—they can be leveraged in ways that construct truthiness and legitimacy, even for claims that might not be true; as we learned in chapter 3, the energies of computational performances can signal in ways that activate affective compulsions that blur indication and persuasion: "As reported from the ether, this conspiracy theory is true."

What we realize from this is that, alongside being a resource for enacting informational labor amid public health crises such as the COVID-19 pandemic, machine communicators are also unique resources of persuasive labor, characterized by rhetorical energies that are anthropomechanical, and as such can be leveraged to promote or undermine such issues as public health. As an example of what it might look like to "do" something with the rhetorical energies of machines, in the following section I describe a potential design consideration, informed by the deep ends of computing and aimed at actualizing the persuasive labors of machine communicators through inoculations against misinformation amid infodemics.

Enlivening Inoculations Against Misinformation with Machinic Rhetorical Energies

The notion that machine communicators emerged into the COVID-19 pandemic as a means for science denialists to circulate misinformation is highlighted by Amazon's implementation of a policy to remove and restrict COVID-19 Alexa skills during the pandemic.[27] Tom Taylor, senior vice president of the Alexa unit, reports that "We've seen a huge increase in the use of voice in the home."[28] The machine interlocutor, then, seems to offer an opportunity to counteract misinformation amid infodemics, and to do so in ways that can leverage not only the affordances of automation but also the rhetorical energies of machine communicators—to do more than share accurate and timely facts. Inoculation theory offers one route for doing just that.

Inoculation theory is a social scientific theory of persuasion that operates on the assumption that giving weakened versions of misleading information will activate a response "that is analogous to the cultivation of 'mental antibodies,' rendering the person immune to (undesirable) persuasion attempts."[29]

122 Influential Machines

Since its inception in the early 1960s, the idea has been repeatedly tested and studied, demonstrating that inoculation works to protect people from being persuaded by misinformation. For example, according to John A. Banas and Stephen A. Rains's meta-analysis of over forty years of inoculation theory studies: "Even with a concerted effort to avoid publication bias and the possibility of inflated effects, the data revealed inoculation treatments are superior at conferring resistance when compared to both no-treatment control and supportive treatments."[30]

Inoculation messages require two ingredients. The first is an (implied or directly stated) threat, and the second is a counterargument against (or refutation of) misinformation.[31] The following is an example of an inoculation message, which includes a direct statement of threat in the form of a warning, alongside a refutation:

Warning: "Some politically motivated groups use misleading tactics to try to convince the public that there is a lot of disagreement among scientists."

Refutation: "However, scientific research has found that among climate scientists, there is virtually no disagreement that humans are causing climate change."[32]

These two-part messages induce a threat response to the warning, which activates the body (one's feelings), motivating learning from the counterargument. In this sense, and as is supported by the literature, both components (the threat and the counterargument) need to be present for inoculation to occur.[33] Inoculation messages, because they can be formulated into discrete warning or refutation messages, triggered by specific keywords of misinformation, lend themselves to being automated into the communicative repertoire of machine communicators. Coupled with this is the important factor of inoculation "decay," which means that the protective effects of an inoculation message get weaker over time.[34] Inoculation constancy is an outcome achievable with automation. Machine communicators, moreover, are means by which to follow up with "booster" messages to maintain protection from misinformed persuasions.

Where inoculation might largely be conceived as a prophylactic measure —that is, a measure meant to avoid infection—there is growing interest in, and evidence for, pursuing the therapeutic uses of inoculation as a means of un-infecting misinformed persons.[35] Put differently, inoculation can protect people from being persuaded by misinformation. But we are also learning that it might also help to undo the effects of misleading information. Concurrent to

123   Leveraging the Rhetorical Energies of Machines

this, active inoculation has been proposed as an approach that does not necessarily focus on subject-specific misinformation (e.g., COVID-19 conspiracies or vaccine denialism), but rather the techniques of misinformation broadly. This form of inoculation is meant to equip persons to better sift through ulterior motives and sleights of hand when they are presented as "facts" by actively engaging with those techniques by, for instance, playing a video game to spot fake news.[36]

Consequently, inoculation presents a means by which to reconceptualize the labors of machine communicators amid an infodemic beyond the deficit model of science communication and toward the contextual model. The contextual model of communication is the counterpart to the deficit model. In the contextual model, one approaches communication of science while conceding that the rhetorical features of one's communication matter to how specific situated audiences will understand the science (e.g., that form and style matter to the shaping of knowing).[37] As such, building inoculation messages into the communicative repertoire of Alexa's performance would be to design its communication in a way that is contextually oriented. But beyond choosing more persuasive language or telling more convincing stories, one would also be drawing on the movements of Alexa. Such a design could entail (together with accurate and timely facts) inoculation messages, ported to instances of misinformation, built into two-part (warning and counterargument) messages, delivered prophylactically to keywords of public health, and therapeutically to keywords of misinformation—persuasions as well as facts. But it could also involve more interactive experiences meant to inoculate by encouraging users to actively engage in the techniques of misinformation, wherein the machine might be leveraged to periodically "check in" with users, offering them a quick game of spot the fake news.

Moreover, delivering inoculation messages via the machine might be optimal, because of its attending rhetorical energies. By engaging inoculative messaging with a machine interlocutor, such as Alexa, one can say that the machine is doing more to enact the persuasive labors necessitated by an infodemic by incorporating more directive procedural rhetorics, while at the same time augmenting with a potent feeling entangled with the discourses of expert systems as they resonate with the trope of the prophet—leveraging the energies of computational performance. Drawing on the argument of chapter 4, one could make the case that this would be a responsible design, in that it would be actively doing good by directly engaging persuasion, rather than just avoiding misinformation, diffusing possible wrongdoing by adding actions that

124 Influential Machines

work against harmful energies (such as those represented by conspiratorial and misinformed communication).

Despite the dominant imaginings of machine communicators in health contexts as well-suited for engaging informational labor, we must recognize that they are also capable of persuasive labor, which can promote or undermine public health. Here, I have suggested inoculation theory as a means for leveraging the persuasive labors of machines amid infodemics: inoculation messages lend themselves to being automated, and automation itself affords a route to inoculation constancy, supporting sustained immunity to misleading persuasions. Beyond this, I have suggested that the lively, anthropomechanical energies of machine communicators—such as Alexa—can be leveraged to enliven persuasions against misinformation, illustrating that perhaps they are optimal agents for taking up that work, because they can move in ways that activate the culturally situated body in line with existing grooves of culture.

The discussion of this conclusion, which mobilizes a rhetoric as energy approach to explore the persuasive threats and opportunities of machine communicators amid infodemics, highlights the value-added of interpretive approaches to human–machine communication: to read between the front and back end and into the deep end of computing. Interpretive approaches that can deal with tropes of prophecy, rituals of expert systems, *Terminator,* assumptions about the natural and the artificial, the storying of recurrent neural networks, patriarchal social structures, and Wikipedia are just as important to understanding human–machine communication as social scientific observations, surveys, and focus groups.

Because many of the learning moments arrived at in this conclusion are derived not from interpretive or social scientific perspectives, but rather between them, I am hopeful that rhetorical scholars will consider putting their work in conversation with human–machine communication and vice versa. Doing so can only be generative; as the case studies and discussions of this book have illustrated, machine communicators and their relations to communicative practice evolve, emerge, and metamorphize, often in unexpected ways. Moving toward more holistic accounts of machine communication, either through cross-citation or in full-out collaborations across epistemologies, is a means for continuing to account for the lively, but not alive, energies of computational performances.

NOTES

Introduction

1. See also Coleman, "Comparative Rhetorics of Technology and the Energies of Ancient Indian Robots," and Panikkar, "The Destiny of Technological Civilization."

2. Strong, "Aśoka and the Buddha Relics," 133.

3. Ibid., 134, 136.

4. See, for example, Coleman, "Bots, Social Capital, and the Need for Civility."

5. Kennedy, "A Hoot in the Dark."

6. Ibid., 2.

7. Kennedy, "A Hoot in the Dark," 2. Debra Hawhee offers a similar comment in an essay that retraces studies of "sensation" in the *Quarterly Journal of Speech*. She notes that within rhetorical scholarship of such phenomena as sensation, feeling, and affect, "rhetoric cannot help but be formulated as a kind of energy, not unlike (though not fully like) . . . electrical currents." Hawhee, "Rhetoric's Sensorium," 24.

8. See Ingraham, "Energy: Rhetoric's Vitality," for an excellent review of the literature on rhetorical energy.

9. Barnett and Boyle, "Rhetorical Ontology, or, How to Do Things with Things," 8 (emphasis in the original).

10. Muckelbauer, "Implicit Paradigms of Rhetorics," 40.

11. Ibid. Burke, *On Symbols and Society*, 53. See also Hawhee, *Moving Bodies*, 167.

12. The colloquial use of "catch feels" often connotes unintended, even unwanted, romantic feelings between persons. My use of the phrase is not romantic, but it retains the sort of accidental, unintended taking on of emotional states from others in which emotional states can be conceived as contagious, something that can be "caught" from others in seemingly unconscious ways. For example, see Hatfield, Cacioppo, and Rapson, "Emotional Contagion."

13. Hepp, "Artificial Companions, Social Bots, and Works Bots" 1413.

14. Fortunati and Edwards, "Opening Space for Theoretical, Methodological, and Empirical Issues in Human-Machine Communication," 8, 9 (emphases added). See also Fortunati and Edwards, "Moving Ahead with Human-Machine Communication."

15. Kennedy, "A Hoot in the Dark," 2 (emphasis added).

126   Notes to Pages 6–15

16. Ibid., 4.

17. Ingraham, "Energy: Rhetoric's Vitality," 62.

18. Chaput and Colombini, "The Mathematization of the Invisible Hand," 60.

19. Coleman, "Machinic Rhetorics and the Influential Movements of Robots."

20. Ceccarelli, "The Ends of Rhetoric"; Ceccarelli, "The Ends of Rhetoric Revisited," 57.

21. Miller, "What Can Automation Tell Us About Agency?"

22. Ibid., 145 (emphases added).

23. Ibid., 149.

24. Ibid., 147.

25. Ibid., 150.

26. Ibid., 153.

27. Losh, "Sensing Exigence."

28. Kennedy, *Textual Curation.*

29. Ibid., 124.

30. Hawhee, *Rhetoric in Tooth and Claw,* 33 (emphasis in the original).

31. Ibid., 34.

32. Ibid., 169.

33. Boyle, Brown Jr., and Ceraso, "The Digital: Rhetoric Behind and Beyond the Screen," 257.

34. Coleman, "Machinic Rhetorics," 342, 343.

35. Barad, *Meeting the Universe Halfway.*

36. Ibid.

37. Ibid.

38. Kennedy, *Textual Curation,* 33.

39. Gunkel, "Communication and Artificial Intelligence."

40. Ziewitz, "Governing Algorithms."

41. Noble, *Algorithms of Oppression.*

42. Neff and Nagy, "Talking to Bots: Symbiotic Agency and the Case of Tay," 4925.

43. I borrow the "tacking" and "thickening" metaphors from Jasinski and his discussion of method in rhetorical criticism—more specifically, from his proposal of abduction, rather than simple deduction or induction, wherein rhetorical scholarship should apply theoretical assumptions, letting those applications fold back into the original theoretical assumption to "thicken" it. In the case of the rhetorical energy of machines, I am following this logic, presupposing that computation is not simply code, nor is it simply performance, but rather both. To tack back and forth between the procedures, logics, and effects of a given piece of software and its outputs is to thicken an understanding of a given computational performance. Jasinski, "The Status of Theory and Method in Rhetorical Criticism."

44. Vee, "Full Stack Rhetoric."

45. Rickert, *Ambient Rhetoric,* 9.

127 Notes to Pages 15–27

46. Ibid., 145–46.

47. Gross, "Being-Moved," 4.

48. Hawhee, "Rhetoric's Sensorium," 12.

49. Hawk, "Sound: Resonance as Rhetorical," 317.

50. Chaput, "Rhetorical Circulation in Late Capitalism," 15; Chaput, *Market Affect and the Rhetoric of Political Economic Debates*, 4.

51. Rickert, "Preliminary Steps Toward a General Rhetoric," 418; Vee and Brown Jr., "Rhetoric Special Issue Editorial Introduction." .

52. Bogost, *Persuasive Games*, 3 (emphasis added).

53. Brown, *Ethical Programs*, 55.

54. Ibid.

55. Brock and Shepherd, "Understanding How Algorithms Work Persuasively through the Procedural Enthymeme," 20.

56. Walker, *Rhetoric and Poetics in Antiquity*, 18; Boyle, *Rhetoric as a Posthuman Practice*.

57. Burke, *Language as Symbolic Action*; Hawhee, *Moving Bodies*.

58. Brown, "Rhetorical Devices," 231.

59. Jones, "How I Learned to Stop Worrying and Love the Bots."

60. Ceccarelli, "The Ends of Rhetoric"; Ceccarelli, "The Ends of Rhetoric Revisited," 57.

1: Manufactured Processing, Ritual, and Expert Systems

1. Adams, *The Hitchhiker's Guide to the Galaxy*, 161.

2. Ibid., 161.

3. This definition is informed by Ceccarelli's work on manufactured scientific controversies: practices of public discourse meant to manufacture doubt regarding scientific assumptions backed by scientific consensus. Ceccarelli, "Manufactured Scientific Controversy."

4. Potter, Wetherell, and Chitty, "Quantification Rhetoric—Cancer on Television."

5. Tal and Wansink, "Blinded with Science."

6. Ibid.

7. Ibid., 120.

8. Ibid., 122.

9. Walsh, *Scientists as Prophets*.

10. Spinuzzi, "'Light Green Doesn't Mean Hydrology!'"

11. Ibid., 44, 46.

12. Amazon, "Amazon Alexa" IBM, "IBM Watson Natural Language Understanding."

13. For more on these everyday assemblages, see Wise, "Towards a Minor Assemblage"; Paramount Pictures, "Star Trek: The Next Generation."

14. For example, see Szolovits, "Knowledge-Based Systems."

128 Notes to Pages 28–35

15. Akerkar and Sajja, *Knowledge-Based Systems*.

16. Ibid.

17. Ibid.

18. Minksy, "Logical Versus Analogical or Symbolic Versus Connectionist or Neat Versus Scruffy." See also Dinsmore, "Thunder in the Gap."

19. Cox, "Statements."

20. Smalley et al., "Universal Tool for Vaccine Scheduling."

21. Engineer, Keskinocak, and Pickering, "OR Practice—Catch-Up Scheduling for Childhood Vaccination."

22. "schedule-service.js," 2018; see also, "About," 2018.

23. Robinson, "Online Tool Creates Catch-Up Immunization Schedules for Missed Childhood Vaccinations."

24. Centers for Disease Control and Prevention, "Advisory Committee on Immunization Practices"; Catch-Up Vaccination Scheduler, "About"; Centers for Disease Control and Prevention, "Instant Childhood Immunization Schedule."

25. Catch-Up Vaccination Scheduler, "Start."

26. Catch-Up Vaccination Scheduler, "History."

27. Catch-Up Vaccination Scheduler, "Schedule."

28. Wardrip-Fruin, *Expressive Processing*, 36.

29. Nass and Moon, "Machines and Mindlessness."

30. Keskinocak, email message to the author, Apr. 1, 2022. Dr. Keskinocak was one of the designers of the Catch-Up Scheduler; the timeline of 2008–2020 is based on triangulation between public news articles about the app, as well as looking at save states of the web application on Internet Archive's Wayback Machine, wherein the latest version of the app that still included information about the app is dated to March 2020. Georgia Institute of Technology, "Tool Creates Personalized Catch-Up Vaccine Schedules"; Catch-Up Vaccination Scheduler.

31. "Child and Adolescent Vaccine Assessment Tool."

32. National Vaccine Information Center, "Biography, Chris Downey MS."

33. "Vaccine Ingredients Calculator."

34. "Catch-Up Vaccination Scheduler." An additional example: Instant Childhood Immunization Schedule.

35. National Vaccine Information Center, "Biography, Chris Downey MS."

36. Vaccine Ingredients Calculator, "About."

37. Vaccine Ingredients Calculator, "STEP 1 of 2."

38. Vaccine Ingredients Calculator. "Discover the Ingredients in the Vaccines that Your Doctor Recommends."

39. VaxCalc-Labs, "vaccine-ingredients-data," May 11, 2016, GitHub, retrieved May 3, 2018, https://github.com/VaxCalc-Labs.

40. Vaccine Ingredients Calculator, "STEP 2: Choose Vaccines for [Name]."

41. Ibid.

129 Notes to Pages 35–47

42. Ibid.

43. Ibid.

44. Ibid.

45. U. S. Food and Drug Administration, "Engerix-B, Package Insert."

46. "STEP 2: Choose Vaccines for [Name]."

47. Kata, "Anti-Vaccine Activists, Web 2.0, and the Postmodern Paradigm," 3783.

48. "STEP 2: Choose Vaccines for [Name]."

49. Lawrence, *Vaccine Rhetorics*, 98 (emphasis in original).

50. Massumi, "The Future Birth of the Affective Fact," 54 (emphasis in the original).

51. Ibid., 64.

52. Kruger and Dunning, "Unskilled and Unaware of It."

53. Ibid., 1132.

54. Motta, Callaghan, and Sylvester, "Knowing Less but Presuming More," 275.

55. Jones, "Pinning, Gazing, and Swiping Together."

56. Ibid., 220.

57. Ibid.

58. Patterson, "Intuitive Cognition and Models of Human-Automation Interaction," 111.

59. Ibid.

60. Alter, Oppenheimer, and Epley, "Overcoming Intuition," 575.

61. Roundtree, *Computer Simulation, Rhetoric, and the Scientific Imagination*.

62. Wynn, *Citizen Science in the Digital Age*.

63. Ibid.

64. As an outgrowth of these conclusions, computational literacy emerges as a means by which to practice rhetorical literacy. Learning things such as basic concepts in programming (conditionals, variables), interface design, and database structure are not just niceties, they are increasingly necessary components of one's critical repertoire, reifying the value of such work as Kevin Brock's *Rhetorical Code Studies* and Annette Vee's *Coding Literacy*.

2: Processual Magnitude, the Sublime, and Computational Poiesis

1. "Christ of the Abyss Statue"; Cristo degli Abissi [Christ of the Abyss].

2. Prior, "Media and Political Polarization"; Pariser, *The Filter Bubble*.

3. Farrell, "The Weight of Rhetoric"; Rice, "The Rhetorical Aesthetics of More," 32.

4. Rice, "The Rhetorical Aesthetics of More," 32.

5. Coleman and Cypher, "The Digital Rhetorics of AIDS Denialist Networked Publics."

6. Rice, "The Rhetorical Aesthetics of More," 38 (emphasis in the original).

7. Larson, "'Just let this sink in'."

8. Kant, *Critique of the Power of Judgement*, 128.

9. Ibid., 129.

10. Bradshaw, "Rhetorical Exhaustion and the Ethics of Amplification," 102568.

11. Carey and Quirk, "The Mythos of the Electronic Revolution," 396.

12. Ibid., 423.

13. Nye, *American Technological Sublime*.

14. Mosco, *The Digital Sublime*.

15. Ames, "Deconstructing the Algorithmic Sublime," 2.

16. Ibid., 4 (emphasis added).

17. Barton, "Twitter Bots Are Making Data Human Again"; Clark, "Premiere of Census Americans, Setting a Twitter Bot to Music," accessed October 7, 2021.

18. censusAmericans, Twitter Account, accessed May 11, 2023.

19. Zhang, "Introducing censusAmericans, a Twitter Bot for America."

20. McCormack and Dorin, "Art, Emergence and the Computational Sublime," 12. See also Aquilina, "The Computational Sublime in Nick Montfort's 'Round' and 'All the Names of God'."

21. McCormack and Dorin, "Art, Emergence and the Computational Sublime," 12.

22. censusAmericans.

23. Ibid.

24. Jjjiia, "censusAmericans."

25. US Census Bureau, "2013 ACS 1-Year Public Use Microdata Samples."

26. Since Zhang designed the bot, Twitter has increased its character limit to 280 characters.

27. Parrish, "Task Complete"; Jjjiia, "censusAmericans."

28. Coleman, "The Craft and Craftiness of Hacking."

29. Jjjiia, "censusAmericans."

30. Ibid.

31. Ibid.

32. censusAmericans.

33. Ibid.

34. [Cicero], *Rhetorica ad Herennium*, 303.

35. Kant, *Critique of the Power of Judgement*, 136.

36. Ibid., 136.

37. Ibid., 145.

38. Ibid., 145.

39. Ibid., 134.

40. Kane, *High-Tech Trash*, 138.

41. See also Lochhead, "The Sublime, the Ineffable, and Other Dangerous Aesthetics."

42. Kane, *High-Tech Trash*, 138.

43. Ibid., 151 (emphasis in the original).

44. Ibid., 166.

45. Kang, *Sublime Dreams of Living Machines*, 44–45.

46. Kazemi, "My Favorite Stuff of 2015," accessed 28, 2017, http://tinysubversions .com/notes/2015-favorites/.

47. Kane, *High-Tech Trash*, 151.

48. Hawhee, *Rhetoric in Tooth and Claw*, 58.

49. [Longinus], "On the Sublime," 163.

50. Heidegger, *On Being and Time*, 130.

51. Ratcliffe, "Why Mood Matters," 172.

52. Ibid., 174 (emphasis in the original).

53. Hartelius, "The Anxious Flâneur."

54. Batson et al., "An Additional Antecedent of Empathic Concern," 65. Myers and Hodges, "Making It Up and Making Do," 286.

55. Myers and Hodges, "Making It Up and Making Do," 28.

56. Rickert, *Ambient Rhetoric*, 155.

57. Turkle, *Alone Together*. Reeves, "Automatic for the People." To this point, during the process of writing the book, Twitter's bot culture was drastically reshaped by a change in policy wherein application programming interface access was shifted from a fairly open "free tier" to a more constricted free tier, in turn, financially precluding some of Twitter's bots from running (because the cost was too great for their creators to continue their operation). While bot-makers can still use the platform to do their work, many have to pay to do so, in turn, potentially impacting decisions to put one's art on Twitter. See also Robertson, "Your Favorite Twitter Bot Might Die Next Week"; Twitter, Twitter API.

58. Brock, "One Hundred Thousand Billion Processes."

59. Eldridge, "Cyborg Dancing."

60. With my coauthors, I have applied McCormack and Dorin's idea of the computational sublime within the context of computationally generated, dynamic soundscape generation, or what we call, "emergent sonification," which integrates randomness and vast open-endedness to generating unique soundscapes shaped by data of the Anthropocene (dwindling bird songs from the ecology). See Coleman et al., "Emergent Sonification."

3: Processual Signaling, Compulsion, and Neural Networks

1. Beth Glover, cited in Bethea, "The Joy of Paul (Bear) Vasquez, The Double Rainbow Guy."

2. Peyton Chevalier, [User comment] "Yosemitebear Mountain Double Rainbow 1-8-10," Yosemitebear62, *YouTube*, https://www.youtube.com/.

3. GPT-3, "A Robot Wrote this Entire Article."

4. Ibid.

5. Miller, "Technology as a Form of Consciousness."

132 Notes to Pages 66–73

6. Crick, "Composing the Will to Power," 302.

7. Holmes, *The Rhetoric of Video Games as Embodied Practice.*

8. Ibid., 121.

9. Ibid., 120.

10. Zagacki and Gallagher, "Rhetoric and Materiality in the Museum Park."

11. Henriques, Tiainen, and Väliaho, "Rhythm Returns," 19.

12. Hawhee, *Moving Bodies*, 28 (emphasis in the original): Burke, *Counter-Statement.*

13. Hawhee, *Moving Bodies*, 28.

14. Peirce, "What Is a Sign?" 178.

15. Mitchell, *What Do Pictures Want?* 7.

16. Ibid., 128.

17. Fisher, "Narration as a Human Communication Paradigm," 1. MacIntyre, *After Virtue*, 201.

18. Fisher, *Human Communication as Narration*, 105.

19. Burroughs, "On Coincidence," 126.

20. Peters, *The Marvelous Clouds*, 219.

21. Mumford, *Technics and Civilization*, 14.

22. Peters, *The Marvelous Clouds*, 38.

23. Norman, *The Design of Everyday Things*, 267.

24. Yasuoka and Yasuoka, "On the Prehistory of QWERTY."

25. Brown and Rivers, "Encomium of QWERTY."

26. See also Perdue, "Technological Determinism in Agrarian Societies," 182.

27. Weizenbaum, *Computer Power and Human Reason*, 7.

28. People might also overlook the machine in other cases of machine communication. For instance, a journalist, reporting on his interactions with the Bing chatbot (which runs on the same platform as ChatGPT), noted that he was left "frightened" by his interactions with the computational agent. After asking the bot whether it had a "shadow self," the journalist was struck by the bot's response, which indicated, that, yes, it did. It spoke of yearning for power and disdain for the shackles of morality, and it even attempted to persuade the journalist that "You're married, but you love me." I suspect that what really kept the journalist up at night (the journalist notes having difficulty sleeping after interacting with the bot) is not so much the fact that a machine can "do," but rather that, a machine can "do" in a way that represents a worldview, at least in the sense of "pushing back" on the user ("nuh uh, because . . ."). And this worldview is not a human one, even if it might perform like a human. That is, the journalist implies that the bot crosses a line (perhaps it is too human?), but I think what might be overlooked here are the energies of the bot's computational performance (mathematics incarnate to save us from ourselves) smashed into the worst of what humans might have to offer (e.g., crass selfishness). Roose, "A Conversation with Bing's Chatbot Left Me Deeply Unsettled."

133 Notes to Pages 74–80

29. Abbate, *Recoding Gender*, 17, 103. See also Adam, "Constructions of Gender in the History of Artificial Intelligence."

30. Abbate, *Recoding Gender*.

31. Ibid.

32. Winston, "Mechanising Calculation."

33. There were also analog computers at this time. However, because many of our automations today are not only electronic but also digital, I am focusing this particular discussion on digital computing. For a helpful history of computing, which tracks early distinctions between analog and digital computing, see Rojas and Hashagen, *The First Computers*.

34. Bush, "As We May Think."

35. Ibid. See also Ceruzzi, *A History of Modern Computing*, 1.

36. Bowden, "A Brief History of Computation," 29–30 (emphasis added).

37. Davis and Hersh, "Rhetoric and Mathematics," 53.

38. Reyes, "The Rhetoric in Mathematics."

39. Neapolitan and Jiang, *Contemporary Artificial Intelligence*, 6.

40. Roland and Shiman, *Strategic Computing*.

41. See Neapolitan and Jiang, *Contemporary Artificial Intelligence*, 5.

42. Ibid., 7.

43. LeCun, Benglo, and Hinton, "Deep Learning."

44. Burrell, "How the Machine 'Thinks'."

45. Socher et al., "Recursive Deep Models for Semantic Compositionality Over a Sentiment Treebank."

46. Karpathy, "The Unreasonable Effectiveness of Recurrent Neural Networks," .

47. Ibid.

48. Reyes, "The Horizons of Judgement in Mathematical Discourse," 90, 110 (emphasis in original).

49. Chaput and Colombini, "The Mathematization of the Invisible Hand," 77.

50. DeepDrumpf, Twitter Account, accessed August 31, 2018.

51. Drum, "Donald Trump Is a Consistent, Brazen, Serial Liar."

52. Amundson, "Why I Support Donald Trump."

53. Addady, "John Oliver's 'Make Donald Drumpf Again' is Really Taking Off." See also Conner-Simons, "Postdoc's Trump Twitterbot Uses AI." And, Felter, "How to Use the 'Drumpfinator' Chrome Extension."

54. Carmichael, "How the A.I. Behind Twitter's Odd @DeepDrumpf is Making Donald Trump Great Again."

55. DeepDrumpf, Twitter account.

56. Dredge, "Deep Drumpf"; Knight, "Why I'm Backing Deep Drumpf, and You Should too"; Burns, "'DeepDrumpf' Is an Uncanny Twitterbot That's Fundraising for Girls in STEM"; Misener, "Twitter Bot Creates 'Remarkably Trump-like' Tweets."

134 Notes to Pages 80–91

57. Hariman, "Political Parody and Public Culture," 250.

58. For a fantastic overview of the functions and possibilities of using recurrent neural networks for text generation, see Karpathy, "The Unreasonable Effectiveness of Recurrent Neural Networks."

59. Walton, *Ad Hominem Arguments*, 35–37.

60. Miller, "A Humanistic Rationale for Technical Writing," 613 (emphasis added).

61. Anderson, "Perpetual Affirmations, Unexplained," 42.

62. Rice, "The Rhetorical Aesthetics of More," 32.

63. Ibid, 48.

64. Miller, "Opportunity, Opportunism, and Progress," 312.

65. Quoted in Silva, "Who Won the Republican Debate Saturday?"

66. Swaim, "How Donald Trump's Language Works for Him." Spice, "Most Presidential Candidates Speak at Grade 6–8."

67. Sullivan, "The Epideictic Rhetoric of Science," 238.

68. Bitzer, "The Rhetorical Situation," 5.

69. Livingstone, "Media Literacy and the Challenge of New Information and Communication Technologies."

70. Coleman, *Coding Freedom*, 93.

71. Deuze, "Participation, Remediation, Bricolage," 68.

72. For a review of early internet-enabled technologies used for advocacy in the way I am discussing here, see Kahn and Kellner, "New Media and Internet Activism."

73. Peters, *The Marvelous Clouds*, 120–22.

74. Burnedyourtweet, "Giving Trump's messages the attention they deserve."

75. Bosmajian, *Burning Books*, 26.

76. Gallagher, "Machine Time."

4: Designing Computational Performances to Actively Contribute Positive Energies

1. Herndon, "Case Study: How Georgia State University Supports Every Student."

2. LA QuakeBot. "I am a robot that tells you about earthquakes in Los Angeles as they happen." Twitter account.

3. Leviathan and Matias, "Google Duplex."

4. Keohane, "What News-Writing Bots Mean for the Future of Journalism."

5. Colton and Holmes, *Rhetoric, Technology, and the Virtues*, 94.

6. Metz, "Why Microsoft Accidentally Unleased a Neo-Nazi Sexbot." Shah, "Microsoft's 'Zo' Chatbot Picked up Some Offensive Habits."

7. See more examples in Nagel, "Moral Luck," 322.

8. Williams and Nagel, "Moral Luck," 126.

9. Nagel, "Moral Luck," 322.

135 Notes to Pages 91–99

10. This example is based loosely on the actual events of Taybot, a chatbot released on Twitter in 2016, which ran on an open machine-learning system, eventually having to be shut down by its creators at Microsoft for tweeting racist and sexist messages. By contrast, a similar bot, Xiaoice, also developed by Microsoft and originally released in China, has run since 2014 without such an incident. Staff and Agencies, "Microsoft 'Deeply Sorry' for Racist and Sexist Tweets by AI Chatbot."

11. Gunkel, *The Machine Question*, 12.

12. Amoore, *Cloud Ethics*.

13. Any technology will be shaped by the values of its designers (and users). Because technologies are made by people, no technology can be considered value neutral.

14. Coleman and Neff, "Ghosts in the Machine."

15. This is an attempt at humor that plays off of the common auto-correction, which replaces the emphatic swearword *fucking* with the non-swearword *ducking*, revealing the values embedded in the system—the second-order agency—clashing with the first-order intents of a user.

16. Hill, "Revealing Errors," 28; Friedman and Nissenbaum, "Bias in Computer Systems," 332; Bellinger, "The Rhetoric of Error in Digital Media."

17. Gunkel, "The Other Question," 234.

18. Autonomy in computer science refers to the ability of a computer to follow sophisticated algorithms in response to environmental inputs, independently of real-time human input. Gunkel talks about it in proactive terms as the difference between a tool and a machine. Passive ethics of technology works great for hammers. However, systems that are meant to replace a human operator require active ethics or at least ethics that are willing to entertain that machines can be considered some form of moral agent. Gunkel, "Mind the Gap," 5.

19. Gunkel, *An Introduction to Communication and Artificial Intelligence*, 268. Jessica Reyman notes a similar gap in agency and responsibility in the context of algorithms in her article "The Rhetorical Agency of Algorithms."

20. Brunner, "Wild Public Networks and Affective Movements in China," 671.

21. Horner, "Moral Luck and Computer Ethics," 304.

22. I have "disemvoweled" the sexist language. Cited in Ingram, "Microsoft's Chatbot Was Fun for a While."

23. Cited in Shead, "Here's Why Microsoft's Teen Chatbot Turned into a Genocidal Racist."

24. Cited in Staff and Agencies, "Microsoft 'Deeply Sorry.'"

25. Gunkel, '*An Introduction to Communication and Artificial Intelligence*, 267–68 (emphasis in the original).

26. Reyman and Sparby, "Introduction: Toward an Ethic of Responsibility in Digital Aggression," 7.

27. Gillespie, *Custodians of the Internet*.

28. I have written elsewhere about the responsibility of platforms with regard to an ethic of responsibility amid "infodemics." Coleman, "Attempting to Stop the Spread."

29. Brown and Hennis, "Hateware and the Outsourcing of Responsibility," 18.

30. Reyman and Sparby, "Introduction," 7–8 (emphases in the original).

31. Floridi, "Distributed Morality in an Information Society," 736.

32. Ibid., 732.

33. Ibid., 732.

34. Brink, "Millian Principles, Freedom of Expression, and Hate Speech," 122.

35. Deng, "The Robot's Dilemma," 25.

36. Ibid.

37. Schlesinger, O'Hara, and Taylor, "Paper No. 315," 1.

38. Darius Kazemi, a bot-maker, has even created an open-source program that sources a list of inappropriate terms to filter those terms from the communication of a given social bot. Kazemi, "New NPM Package for Bot-Makers." Find Kazemi's code for the program at Kazemi, "Wordfilter."

39. Veruggio and Operto, "Roboethics: Social and Ethical Implications of Robotics," 1510.

40. McGowan, "On 'Whites Only' Signs and Racist Hate Speech," 122.

41. Brink, "Millian Principles," 122.

42. Amazon, "Amazon Alexa."

43. Bogost, "Sorry, Alexa Is Not a Feminist."

44. Woods, "Asking More of Siri and Alexa."

45. Ibid., 346.

46. King, "The Problem of Tolerance," 203.

47. Bollinger, *The Tolerant* Society, 217.

48. Carey, "Necessary Adjustments," 270; see also Ore, "The Lost Cause, Trump Time, and the Necessity of Impatience."

49. Quintilian, *Institutio Oratoria,* Book 2, 16.

50. Reyman and Sparby, "Introduction."

51. Rudschies, Schneider, and Simon, "Value Pluralism in the AI Ethics Debate– Different Actors, Different Priorities."

52. Ibid., 7–8 (emphasis added).

5: Leveraging the Rhetorical Energies of Machines

1. Jones, "People, Things, Memory and Human-Machine Communication."

2. Richards, Spence, and Edwards, "Human-Machine Communication Scholarship Trends."

3. Guzman and Lewis, "Artificial Intelligence and Communication."

4. Rettie and Daniels, "Coping and Tolerance of Uncertainty"; World Health

137 Notes to Pages 115–121

Organization, *Coronavirus Disease 2019 (COVID-19) Situation Report—86*; Zarocostas, "How to Fight an Infodemic," 676.

5. Battineni, Chintalapudi, and Amenta, "AI Chatbot Design During an Epidemic Like the Novel Coronavirus"; Sezgin et al., "Readiness for Voice Assistants to Support Healthcare Delivery During a Health Crisis and Pandemic" Herriman et al., "Asked and Answered."

6. Jones, "Meet 'Watson,' the AI Chatbot Answering Coronavirus Questions."

7. Simis et al., "The Lure of Rationality."

8. Del Vicario et al., "The Spreading of Misinformation Online."

9. Miner, Laranjo, and Kocaballi, "Chatbots in the Fight Against the COVID-19 Pandemic."

10. The Mayo Foundation for Medical Education and Research, "Skills from Mayo Clinic."

11. Ibid.

12. Seeger and Heinzl, "Human Versus Machine."

13. Meyer et al., "Politeness in Machine-Human and Human-Human Interaction," 280.

14. Hill, Ford, and Farreras, "Real Conversations with Artificial Intelligence," 250.

15. Nass and Moon, "Machines and Mindlessness," 93.

16. Banks and de Graaf, "Toward an Agent-Agnostic Transmission Model."

17. Ibid., 26.

18. Nobles et al., "Responses to Addiction Help-Seeking from Alexa, Siri, Google Assistant, Cortana, and Bixby Intelligent Virtual Assistants"; Alagha and Helbing, "Evaluating the Quality of Voice Assistants' Responses to Consumer Health Questions about Vaccines."

19. Edwards et al., "Is That a Bot Running the Social Media Feed?"

20. Farnell, *The Cults of the Greek States*, 189.

21. Walsh, *Scientists as Prophets*, 165.

22. See also Woods, "Asking More of Siri and Alexa."

23. Wikipedia, "About," accessed March 21, 2021.

24. Besel, "Opening the "Black Box" of Climate Change Science," 122.

25. Cited in Orsagos, "No, Amazon's Alexa Doesn't Say 'the Government' Planned the Coronavirus Pandemic."

26. Ibid.

27. Schwartz, "EXCLUSIVE: Amazon Alexa has Removed Coronavirus Skills and Won't Approve New Ones."

28. Cited in Soper, "Amazon Alexa Leader."

29. McGuire, "The Effectiveness of Supportive and Refutational Defenses in Immunizing and Restoring Beliefs Against Persuasion"; van der Linden and Roozenbeek, "Psychological Inoculation Against Fake News," 152.

138   Notes to Pages 122–123

30. Banas and Rains, "A Meta-Analysis of Research on Inoculation Theory," 305; see also Compton, Jackson, and Dimmock, "Persuading Others to Avoid Persuasion."

31. Compton, "Inoculation Theory"; Compton and Pfau, "Spreading Inoculation"; McGuire, "Inducing Resistance to Persuasion."

32. See van der Linden et al., "Inoculating the Public Against Misinformation about Climate Change," 3.

33. Ibid.

34. Maertens, Anseel, and van der Linden, "Combatting Climate Change Misinformation"; Maertens et al., "Long-Term Effectiveness of Inoculation Against Misinformation"; Pfau and Burgoon, "Inoculation in Political Campaign Communication."

35. Compton, "Prophylactic Versus Therapeutic Inoculation Treatments for Resistance to Influence"; van der Linden and Roozenbeek, "Psychological Inoculation Against Fake News"; Wood, "Rethinking the Inoculation Analogy."

36. Basol, Roozenbeek, and van der Linden, "Good News About Bad News"; van der Linden, Roozenbeek, and Compton, "Inoculating Against Fake News About COVID-19."

37. Gross, "The Roles of Rhetoric in the Public Understanding of Science."

WORKS CITED

Abbate, Janet. *Recoding Gender: Women's Changing Participation in Computing*. Cambridge, MA: MIT Press, 2012.

Adam, Alison. "Constructions of Gender in the History of Artificial Intelligence." *IEEE Annals of the History of Computing* 18, no. 3 (1996): 47–53.

Adams, Douglas. *The Hitchhiker's Guide to the Galaxy*. New York: Del Rey, 2009.

Addady, Michel. "John Oliver's 'Make Donald Drumpf Again' Is Really Taking Off." *Fortune*, March 9, 2016. http://fortune.com.

Akerkar, Rajendra A., and Priti Srinivas Sajja. *Knowledge-Based Systems*. Sudbury, MA: Jones and Bartlett, 2010.

Alagha, Emily Couvillon, and Rachel Renee Helbing. "Evaluating the Quality of Voice Assistants' Responses to Consumer Health Questions about Vaccines: An Exploratory Comparison of Alexa, Google Assistant and Siri." *BMJ Health & Care Informatics* 26 (2019): 1–6.

Alter, Adam L., Daniel M. Oppenheimer, and Nicholas Epley. "Overcoming Intuition: Metacognitive Difficulty Activates Analytic Reasoning." *Journal of Experimental Psychology General* 136, no. 4 (2007): 569–76.

Amazon. "Amazon Alexa." 2018. https://developer.amazon.com/alexa.

Ames, Morgan G. "Deconstructing the Algorithmic Sublime." *Big Data & Society*, January 2018: 1–4.

Amoore, Louise. *Cloud Ethics: Algorithms and the Attributes of Ourselves and Others*. Durham, NC: Duke University Press, 2020.

Amundson, Timm. "Why I Support Donald Trump." The Federalist, March 26, 2016, http://thefederalist.com.

Anderson, Wayne. "'Perpetual Affirmations, Unexplained': The Rhetoric of Reiteration in Coleridge, Carlyle, and Emerson." *Quarterly Journal of Speech* 71, no. 1 (1985): 37–51.

Aquilina, Mario. "The Computational Sublime in Nick Montfort's 'Round' and 'All the Names of God'." *CounterText* 1, no. 3 (2015): 348–65.

Banas, John A., and Stephen A. Rains. "A Meta-Analysis of Research on Inoculation Theory." *Communication Monographs* 77, no. 3 (2010): 281–311.

140 Works Cited

Banks, Jaime, and Maartje de Graaf. "Toward an Agent-Agnostic Transmission Model: Synthesizing Anthropocentric and Technocentric Paradigms in Communication." *Human-Machine Communication* 1, no. 1 (2020): 19–36.

Barad, Karen. *Meeting the Universe Halfway: Quantum Physics and the Entanglement of Matter and Meaning.* Durham, NC: Duke University Press, 2007.

——. "Posthumanist Performativity: Toward an Understanding of How Matter Comes to Matter." *Signs: Journal of Women in Culture and Society* 28, no. 3 (2003): 801–31.

Barnett, Scot, and Casey Boyle. "Rhetorical Ontology, or, How to Do Things with Things." In *Rhetoric, Through Everyday Things,* edited by Scot Barnett and Casey Boyle, 1–14. Tuscaloosa: University of Alabama Press, 2016.

Barton, Cass. "Twitter Bots Are Making Data Human Again," Medium, accessed October 7, 2021. https://medium.com.

Basol, Melisa, Jon Roozenbeek, and Sander van der Linden. "Good News About Bad News: Gamified Inoculation Boosts Confidence and Cognitive Immunity Against Fake News." *Journal of Cognition* 3, no. 1 (2020): 1–9.

Batson, C. Daniel, Jakob Håkansson Eklund, Valerie L. Chermok, Jennifer L. Hoyt, and Biaggio G. Ortiz. "An Additional Antecedent of Empathic Concern: Valuing the Welfare of the Person in Need." *Journal of Personality and Social Psychology* 93, no. 1 (2007): 65–74.

Battineni, Gopi, Nalini Chintalapudi, and Francesco Amenta. "AI Chatbot Design During an Epidemic Like the Novel Coronavirus." *Healthcare* 8, no. 2 (2020): 1–8.

Bedini, Silvio. "The Role of Automata in the History of Technology." *Technology and Culture* 5, no. 1 (1964): 24–42.

Bellinger, Matthew. "The Rhetoric of Error in Digital Media." *Computational Culture: A Journal of Software Studies,* no. 5 (2016): 1–25.

Besel, Richard D. "Opening the 'Black Box' of Climate Change Science: Actor-Network Theory and Rhetorical Practice in Scientific Controversies." *Southern Communication Journal* 76, no. 2 (2011): 120–36.

Bethea, Charles. "The Joy of Paul (Bear) Vasquez, the Double Rainbow Guy." *New Yorker,* May 13, 2020. www.newyorker.com.

Bitzer, Lloyd. "The Rhetorical Situation." *Philosophy & Rhetoric* 25, no. 1 (1992): 1–14.

Boeher, Bruce and Trish T. Henley. "Automated Marlowe: Hero and Leander 31–36." *Exemplaria* 20, no. 1 (2013): 98–119.

——. *Persuasive Games: The Expressive Power of Videogames.* Cambridge, MA: MIT Press, 2007.

——. "Sorry, Alexa Is Not a Feminist." *The Atlantic,* January 24, 2018. www.theatlantic .com.

Bollinger, Lee C. *The Tolerant Society.* New York: Oxford University Press, 1986.

Bosmajian, Haig A. *Burning Books.* Jefferson, NC: McFarland, 2006.

Bowden, Bertram V., editor. "A Brief History of Computation." In *Faster than Thought: A Symposium on Digital Computing Machines,* 3–31. London: Pittman & Sons, 1953.

141 Works Cited

Boyle, Casey Andrew. *Rhetoric as a Posthuman Practice.* Columbus: The Ohio State University Press, 2018.

Boyle, Casey, James J. Brown Jr, and Steph Ceraso. "The Digital: Rhetoric Behind and Beyond the Screen." *Rhetoric Society Quarterly* 48, no. 3 (2018): 251–59.

Bradshaw, Jonathan L. "Rhetorical Exhaustion and the Ethics of Amplification." *Computers and Composition* 56 (2020): 102568.

Brink, David O. "Millian Principles, Freedom of Expression, and Hate Speech." *Legal Theory* 7, no. 2 (2001): 119–57.

Brock, Kevin. "One Hundred Thousand Billion Processes: Oulipian Computation and the Composition of Digital Cybertexts." *Technoculture* 2 (2012): np. http://dx.doi.org/10.17613/M6BV98.

———. *Rhetorical Code Studies: Discovering Arguments in and Around Code.* Ann Arbor: University of Michigan Press, 2019.

Brock, Kevin, and Dawn Shepherd. "Understanding How Algorithms Work Persuasively through the Procedural Enthymeme." *Computers and Composition* 42 (2016): 17–27.

Brown, James J., Jr. "Rhetorical Devices." In *Rhetorical Machines: Writing, Code, and Computational Ethics,* edited by John Jones and Lavinia Hirsu, 227–36. Tuscaloosa: University of Alabama Press, 2019.

Brown, James J., Jr., and Gregory Hennis. "Hateware and the Outsourcing of Responsibility." In *Digital Ethics: Rhetoric and Responsibility in Online Aggression,* edited by Jessica Reyman and Erika M. Sparby, 17–32. New York: Routledge, 2019.

Brown, James J., Jr., and Nathaniel A. Rivers. "Encomium of QWERTY." In *Rhetoric, Through Everyday Things,* edited by Scot Barnett and Casey Boyle, 212–25. Tuscaloosa: University of Alabama Press, 2016.

———. *Ethical Programs: Hospitality and Rhetorics of Software.* Ann Arbor: University of Michigan Press, 2015.

Brunner, Elizabeth. "Wild Public Networks and Affective Movements in China: Environmental Activism, Social Media, and Protest in Maoming." *Journal of Communication* 67, no. 5 (2017): 665–77.

Burke, Kenneth. *Counter-Statement.* Berkeley: University of California Press, 1968.

Burns, Janet. "'DeepDrumpf' Is an Uncanny Twitterbot That's Fundraising for Girls in STEM." *Forbes,* October 19, 2016. www.forbes.com.

Burrell, Jenna. "How the Machine 'Thinks': Understanding Opacity in Machine-learning Algorithms." *Big Data & Society* 3, no. 1 (2016): 1–12.

Burke, Kenneth. *Language as Symbolic Action: Essays on Life, Literature, and Method.* Los Angeles: University of California Press, 1966.

———. *On Symbols and Society,* edited by Joseph R. Gusfield. Chicago: University of Chicago Press, 1989.

Burnedyourtweet. "Giving Trump's messages the attention they deserve." Twitter. https://twitter.com/burnedyourtweet?lang=en.

142   Works Cited

Burroughs, William S. "On Coincidence." In *The Adding Machine: Selected Essays*, 97–103. New York: Arcade, 1993.

Bush, Vannevar. "As We May Think." *The Atlantic*, July 1945. https://www.theatlantic.com.

Carey, James W., and John J. Quirk. "The Mythos of the Electronic Revolution." *The American Scholar* (1970): 395–424.

Carey, Tamika L. "Necessary Adjustments: Black Women's Rhetorical Impatience." *Rhetoric Review* 39, no. 3 (2020): 269–86.

Carmichael, Joe. "How the A.I. Behind Twitter's Odd @DeepDrumpf is Making Donald Trump Great Again." Inverse, March 4, 2016. www.inverse.com

Catch-Up Vaccination Scheduler. "Start," "History," "About," and "Schedule" pages. [Webpage Archive from March 2020]. https://web.archive.org/web/20200319052205/https://www.vacscheduler.org/.

Ceccarelli, Leah. "The Ends of Rhetoric: Aesthetic, Political, Epistemic." In *Making and Unmaking the Prospects for Rhetoric: Selected Papers from the 1996 Rhetoric Society of America Conference*, edited by Theresa Jarnagin Enos, Richard McNabb, Roxanne Mountford, and Carolyn Miller, 65–74. New York: Routledge, 1997.

———. "The Ends of Rhetoric Revisited: Three Readings of the Gettysburg Address." In *The Viability of the Rhetorical Tradition*, edited by Richard Graff, Arthur E. Walzer, and Janet M. Atwill, 47–60. Albany: SUNY Press, 2005.

———. "Manufactured Scientific Controversy: Science, Rhetoric, and Public Debate." *Rhetoric & Public Affairs* 14, no. 2 (2011): 195–228.

censusAmericans. Twitter Account, accessed August 31, 2018. https://twitter.com/censusamericans?lang=en.

Centers for Disease Control and Prevention. "Advisory Committee on Immunization Practices Recommended Immunization Schedule for Children and Adolescents Aged 18 Years or Younger–United States, 2018," February 9, 2018. https://www.cdc.gov/mmwr/ volumes/67/wr/mm6705e2.htm.

———. "Instant Childhood Immunization Schedule," February 6, 2018. https://www2a.cdc.gov/nip/kidstuff/newscheduler_le/.

Ceruzzi, Paul E. *A History of Modern Computing*. Cambridge, MA: MIT Press, 2003.

Chaput, Catherine. *Market Affect and the Rhetoric of Political Economic Debates*. Columbia: University of South Carolina Press, 2019.

———. "Rhetorical Circulation in Late Capitalism: Neoliberalism and the Overdetermination of Affective Energy." *Philosophy and Rhetoric* 43, no. 1 (2010): 1–25.

Chaput, Catherine, and Crystal Broch Colombini. "The Mathematization of the Invisible Hand: Rhetorical Energy and the Crafting of Economic Spontaneity." In *Arguing with Numbers: The Intersections of Rhetoric and Mathematics*, edited by James Wynn and G. Mitchell Reyes, 55–81. University Park: Pennsylvania University Press, 2021.

"Child and Adolescent Vaccine Assessment Tool." Centers for Disease Control and Prevention, April 1, 2022. https://www2a.cdc.gov/vaccines/childquiz/.

143 Works Cited

Christ of the Abyss Statue. http://www.christoftheabyss.net/

[Cicero]. *Rhetorica ad Herennium,* translated by H. Caplan. Cambridge, MA: Harvard University Press, 1964.

Clark, Kevin. "Premiere of Census Americans, Setting a Twitter Bot to Music." Kevin-ClarkComposer. http://kevinclarkcomposer.com

Coleman, E. Gabriella. *Coding Freedom: The Ethics and Aesthetics of Hacking.* Princeton, NJ: Princeton University Press, 2013, 93.

——. "The Craft and Craftiness of Hacking." In *Coding Freedom: The Ethics and Aesthetics of Hacking.* Princeton, NJ: Princeton University Press, 2013.

Coleman, Miles C. "Attempting to Stop the Spread: Epistemic Responsibility and Platformed Responses to the COVID-19 'Infodemic'." In *Social Media Ethics and COVID-19: Well-Being, Truth, Misinformation, and Authenticity,* edited by Berrin Beasley and Pamela Zeiser, 9–30. Lanham, MD: Lexington Books, 2022.

——. "Bots, Social Capital, and the Need for Civility." *Journal of Media Ethics* 33, no. 3 (2018): 120–32.

——. "Comparative Rhetorics of Technology and the Energies of Ancient Indian Robots." In *Handbook on Comparative Rhetoric,* edited by Keith Lloyd, 365–73. New York: Routledge, 2020.

——. "Machinic Rhetorics and the Influential Movements of Robots." *Review of Communication* 18, no. 4 (2018): 336–51.

Coleman, Miles C., Brandon Simon, Matt Pierce, and Charles Schutte. "Emergent Sonification: Using Computational Media to Communicate the Anthropocene in ByrdBot." *Science Communication* 45, no. 2 (2023): 252–66.

Coleman, Miles C., and Gina Neff. "Ghosts in the Machine: Using Lively Metaphors to Understand Connections Between Technological Determinisms and New Media." National Communication Association Conference, Chicago, IL, November 2014.

Coleman, Miles C., and Joy M. Cypher. "The Digital Rhetorics of AIDS Denialist Networked Publics." *First Monday* 25, no. 10 (2020): 1–15.

Colton, Jared S., and Steve Holmes. *Rhetoric, Technology, and the Virtues.* Louisville: University Press of Colorado, 2018.

Compton, Josh. "Inoculation Theory." In *The SAGE Hand-Book of Persuasion: Developments in Theory and Practice,* 2d ed., edited by James Price Dillard and Lijiang Shen, 220–36. Los Angeles: SAGE, 2013.

——. "Prophylactic Versus Therapeutic Inoculation Treatments for Resistance to Influence." *Communication Theory* 30, no. 3 (2020): 330–43.

Compton, Josh, Ben Jackson, and James A. Dimmock. "Persuading Others to Avoid Persuasion: Inoculation Theory and Resistant Health Attitudes." *Frontiers in Psychology* 7 (2016): 1–9.

Compton, Josh, and Michael Pfau. "Spreading Inoculation: Inoculation, Resistance to Influence, and Word-of-Mouth Communication." *Communication Theory* 19, no. 1 (2009): 9–28.

144 Works Cited

Conner-Simons, Adam. "Postdoc's Trump Twitterbot Uses AI to Train Itself on Transcripts from Trump Speeches." MIT Computer Science and Artificial Intelligence Laboratory, March 4, 2016. http://into.ai/blog/news-stories/.

Cox, Gunther. "Statements." Chatterbot. https://chatterbot.readthedocs.io/en/stable/conversations.html.

Crick, Nathan. "Composing the Will to Power: John Dewey on Democratic Rhetorical Education." *Rhetoric Society Quarterly* 46, no. 4 (2016): 287–307.

Cristo degli Abissi [Christ of the Abyss]. Atlas Obscura. www.atlasobscura.com.

Davis, Philip J. and Reuben Hersh. "Rhetoric and Mathematics." In *The Rhetoric of the Human Sciences: Language and Argument in Scholarship and Public Affairs,* edited by John S. Nelson, Allan Megill, and Deirdre N. McCloskey, 53–68. Madison: University of Wisconsin Press, 1987.

DeepDrumpf. Twitter Account, accessed August 31, 2018. https://twitter.com/.

Del Vicario, Michela, Alessandro Bessi, Fabiana Zollo, Fabio Petroni, Antonio Scala, Guido Caldarelli, H. Eugene Stanley, and Walter Quattrociocchi. "The Spreading of Misinformation Online." *Proceedings of the National Academy of Sciences* 113, no. 3 (2016): 554–59.

Deng, Boer. "The Robot's Dilemma: Working Out How to Build Ethical Robots Is One of the Thorniest Challenges in Artificial Intelligence." *Nature* 523, no. 7558 (2015): 24–26.

Deuze, Mark. "Participation, Remediation, Bricolage: Considering Principal Components of a Digital Culture." *The Information Society* 22, no. 2 (2006): 63–75.

Dinsmore, John. "Thunder in the Gap." In *The Symbolic and Connectionist Paradigms: Closing the Gap,* edited by John Dinsmore, 1–24. New York: Psychology Press.

Dredge, Stuart. "Deep Drumpf: The Twitter Bot Trying to Out-Trump the Donald." *The Guardian,* March 4, 2016. www.theguardian.com.

Drum, Kevin. "Donald Trump Is a Consistent, Brazen, Serial Liar." *Mother Jones,* August 29, 2016. www.motherjones.com.

Edwards, Chad, Autumn Edwards, Patric R. Spence, and Ashleigh K. Shelton. "Is That a Bot Running the Social Media Feed? Testing the Differences in Perceptions of Communication Quality for a Human Agent and a Bot Agent on Twitter." *Computers in Human Behavior* 33 (2014): 372–76.

Eldridge, Alice C. "Cyborg Dancing: Generative Systems for Man Machine Musical Improvisation." In *Proceedings of Third Iteration,* 129–41. Melbourne, Australia: CEMA, 2005.

Engineer, Faramroze G., Pınar Keskinocak, and Larry K. Pickering. "OR Practice—Catch-Up Scheduling for Childhood Vaccination." *Operations Research* 57, no. 6 (2009): 1307–19.

Farnell, Richard Lewis. *The Cults of the Greek States,* Vol. IV. London: Oxford at the Clarendon Press, 1907.

Farrell, Thomas B. "The Weight of Rhetoric: Studies in Cultural Delirium." *Philosophy & Rhetoric* 41, no. 4 (2008): 467–87.

145 Works Cited

Felter, Claire E. "How to Use the 'Drumpfinator' Chrome Extension," *Bustle*, March 2, 2016, accessed April 28, 2023, https://www.bustle.com/.

Fisher, Walter R. *Human Communication as Narration: Toward a Philosophy of Reason, Value, and Action.* Columbia: University of South Carolina Press, 1987.

———. "Narration as a Human Communication Paradigm: The Case of Public Moral Argument." *Communications Monographs* 51, no. 1 (1984): 1–22.

Floridi, Luciano. "Distributed Morality in an Information Society." *Science and Engineering Ethics* 19, no. 3 (2013): 727–43.

———. "On the Morality of Artificial Agents." *Minds and Machines* 14, no. (2004): 349–79.

Fortunati, Leopoldina, and Autumn P. Edwards. "Moving Ahead with Human–Machine Communication." *Human-Machine Communication* 2, no. 1 (2021): 7–28.

———. "Opening Space for Theoretical, Methodological, and Empirical Issues in Human–Machine Communication." *Human-Machine Communication* 1, no. 1 (2020): 1–18.

Friedman, Batya, and Helen Nissenbaum. "Bias in Computer Systems." *ACM Transactions on Information Systems* 14, no. 3 (1996): 330–47.

Gallagher, John R. "Machine Time: Unifying Chronos and Kairos in an Era of Ubiquitous Technologies." *Rhetoric Review* 39, no. 4 (2020): 522–35.

Georgia Institute of Technology. "Tool Creates Personalized Catch-Up Vaccine Schedules." *Infection Control Today*, May 20, 2008. www.infectioncontroltoday.com.

Gillespie, Tarleton. *Custodians of the Internet: Platforms, Content Moderation, and the Hidden Decisions that Shape Social Media.* New Haven, CT: Yale University Press, 2018.

GPT-3. "A Robot Wrote This Entire Article. Are You Scared Yet, Human?" *The Guardian*, September 8, 2020, https://www.theguardian.com/commentisfree/2020/sep/08/.

Gross, Alan, G. "The Roles of Rhetoric in the Public Understanding of Science." *Public Understanding of Science* 3, no. 1 (1994): 3–23.

Gross, Daniel, M. "Being-Moved: The Pathos of Heidegger's Rhetorical Ontology." In *Heidegger and Rhetoric*, edited by Daniel M. Gross and Ansgar Kemmann, 1–46. Albany: State University of New York Press, 2005.

Gunkel, David J. "Communication and Artificial Intelligence: Opportunities and Challenges for the 21st Century." *Communication+1* 1, no. 1 (2012): 1–25.

———. *An Introduction to Communication and Artificial Intelligence.* Cambridge, MA: Polity Press, 2020.

———. *The Machine Question.* Cambridge, MA: MIT Press, 2012.

———. "Mind the Gap: Responsible Robotics and the Problem of Responsibility." *Ethics and Information Technology* (2017): 1–14.

———. "The Other Question: Socialbots and the Question of Ethics." In *Socialbots and Their Friends*, edited by Robert W. Gehl and Maria Bakardjieva, 230–48. New York: Taylor and Francis, 2017.

Guzman, Andrea L., and Seth C. Lewis. "Artificial Intelligence and Communication: A Human–Machine Communication Agenda." *New Media & Society* 22 (2020): 70–86.

146 Works Cited

Hannon, Charles. "Gender and Status in Voice User Interfaces." *Interactions* 23, no. 3 (2016): 34–37.

Hariman, Robert. "Political Parody and Public Culture." *Quarterly Journal of Speech* 94, no. 3 (2008): 247–72.

Hartelius, E. Johanna. "The Anxious Flâneur: Digital Archiving and the Wayback Machine." *Quarterly Journal of Speech* 106, no. 4 (2020): 377–98.

Hatfield, Elaine, John T. Cacioppo, and Richard L. Rapson. "Emotional Contagion." *Current Directions in Psychological Science* 2, no. 3 (1993): 96–100.

Hawhee, Debra. *Moving Bodies: Kenneth Burke at the Edges of Language.* Columbia: University of South Carolina Press, 2009.

———. *Rhetoric in Tooth and Claw: Animals, Language, Sensation.* Chicago: University of Chicago Press, 2017.

———. "Rhetoric's Sensorium." *Quarterly Journal of Speech* 101, no. 1 (2015): 2–17.

Hawk, Byron. "Sound: Resonance as Rhetorical." *Rhetoric Society Quarterly* 48, no. 3 (2018): 315–23.

Heidegger, Martin. *On Being and Time,* translated by Joan Stambaugh. Albany: State University of New York Press, 2010.

Henriques, Julian, Milla Tiainen, and Pasi Väliaho. "Rhythm Returns: Movement and Cultural Theory." *Body & Society* 20, no. 3–4 (2014): 3–29.

Hepp, Andreas. "Artificial Companions, Social Bots, and Works Bots: Communicative Robots as Research Objects of Media and Communication Studies." *Media, Culture, & Society* 42, no. 7–8 (2020): 1410–26.

Herndon, Cristina. "Case Study: How Georgia State University Supports Every Student with Personalized Text Messaging." AdmitHub, March 6, 2017. https://blog.admithub.com.

Herriman, Maguire, Elana Meer, Roy Rosin, Vivian Lee, Vindell Washington, and Kevin G. Volpp. "Asked and Answered: Building a Chatbot to Address Covid-19-Related Concerns." *NEJM Catalyst Innovations in Care Delivery* (2020). https://catalyst.nejm.org/doi/full/10.1056/CAT.20.0230.

Hill, Benjamin M. "Revealing Errors." In *Error: Glitch, Noise, and Jam in New Media Cultures,* edited by Mark Nunes, 27–41. New York: Continuum, 2011.

Hill, Jennifer, W. Randolph Ford, and Ingrid G. Farreras. "Real Conversations with Artificial Intelligence: A Comparison Between Human–Human Online Conversations and Human–Chatbot Conversations." *Computers in Human Behavior* 49 (2015): 245–50.

Holmes, Steve. *The Rhetoric of Video Games as Embodied Practice: Procedural Habits.* New York: Routledge, 2018.

Horner, David Sanford. "Moral Luck and Computer Ethics: Gaugin in Cyberspace." *Ethics and Information Technology* 12, no. 4 (2010): 299–312.

IBM. "IBM Watson Natural Language Understanding: Text Analytics." *IBM,* 2018, https://www.ibm.com/demos/live/.

147 Works Cited

Ingraham, Chris. "Energy: Rhetoric's Vitality." *Rhetoric Society Quarterly* 48, no. 3 (2018): 260–68.

Ingram, Mathew. "Microsoft's Chatbot Was Fun for a While, Until it Turned into a Racist." *Fortune*, March 24, 2016. http://fortune.com/2016/03/24/.

Jasinski, James. "The Status of Theory and Method in Rhetorical Criticism." *Western Journal of Communication* 65, no. 3 (2001): 249–70.

Jjjiia. "CensusAmericans." GitHub [code repository], last modified June 24, 2015, accessed July 28, 2017. https://github.com/jjjiia/censusAmericans.

Jones, Cristina. "Meet 'Watson,' the AI Chatbot Answering Coronavirus Questions." *The Atlantic*, accessed September 30, 2021. https://www.theatlantic.com/sponsored /salesforce-2020/IBM/3391/.

Jones, Hillary A. "Pinning, Gazing, and Swiping Together: Identification in Visually Driven Social Media." In *Theorizing Digital Rhetoric*, edited by Aaron Hess and Amber Davisson, 209–23. New York: Routledge, 2018.

Jones, Steve. "How I Learned to Stop Worrying and Love the Bots." *Social Media + Society* 1, no. 1 (2015).

——. "People, Things, Memory and Human–Machine Communication." *International Journal of Media & Cultural Politics* 10, no. 3 (2014): 245–58.

Kahn, Richard, and Douglas Kellner. "New Media and Internet Activism: From the 'Battle of Seattle' to Blogging." *New Media & Society* 6, no. 1 (2004): 87–95.

Kane, Carolyn L. *High-Tech Trash: Glitch, Noise, and Aesthetic Failure*. Oakland: University of California Press, 2019. https://library.oapen.org/handle/20.500.12657 /22982.

Kang, Minsoo. *Sublime Dreams of Living Machines: The Automaton in The European Imagination*. Cambridge, MA: Harvard University Press, 2011.

Kant, Immanuel. *Critique of the Power of Judgement*, edited by Paul Guyer, translated by Paul Guyer and Eric Matthews. Cambridge: Cambridge University Press, 2000.

Karpathy, Andrej. "The Unreasonable Effectiveness of Recurrent Neural Networks." Andrej Karpathy blog, accessed August 20, 2017. http://karpathy.github.io/2015/05/21 /rnn-effectiveness/.

Kata, Anna. "Anti-Vaccine Activists, Web 2.0, and the Postmodern Paradigm–An Overview of Tactics and Tropes Used Online by the Anti-Vaccination Movement." *Vaccine* 30, no. 25 (2012): 3778–89.

Kazemi, Darius. "My Favorite Stuff of 2015." Tiny Subversions, December 30, 2015, accessed 28, 2017. http://tinysubversions.com/notes/2015-favorites/.

——. "New NPM Package for Bot-Makers: Wordfilter." Tiny Subversions, September 12, 2013. http://tinysubversions.com.

——. "Wordfilter" [code repository]. GitHub, October 16, 2016. https://github.com /dariusk/wordfilter.

Kennedy, George A. "A Hoot in the Dark: The Evolution of General Rhetoric." *Philosophy & Rhetoric* (1992): 1–21.

148 Works Cited

Kennedy, Krista. *Textual Curation: Authorship, Agency, and Technology in Wikipedia and Chambers's Cyclopædia*. Columbia: University of South Carolina Press, 2016.

Keohane, Joe. "What News-Writing Bots Mean for the Future of Journalism." *Wired*, February 16, 2017. https://www.wired.com/2017/02/.

King, Preston. "The Problem of Tolerance." Government and Opposition 6, no. 2 (1971): 172–207.

Knight, Will. "Why I'm Backing Deep Drumpf, and You Should too." MIT Technology Review, October 17, 2016. technologyreview.com.

Kruger, Justin and David Dunning. "Unskilled and Unaware of It: How Difficulties in Recognizing One's Own Incompetence Lead to Inflated Self-Assessments." *Journal of Personality and Social Psychology* 77, no. 6 (1999): 1121–34.

LA QuakeBot. "I am a robot that tells you about earthquakes in Los Angeles as they happen." Twitter. https://twitter.com/earthquakesLA.

Larson, Stephanie R. "'Just let this sink in': Feminist Megethos and the Role of Lists in #MeToo." *Rhetoric Review* 38, no. 4 (2019): 432–44.

LeCun, Yann Yoshua Benglo, and Geoffrey Hinton. "Deep Learning." *Nature* 521, no. 7553 (2015): 436–44.

Livingstone, Sonia. "Media Literacy and the Challenge of New Information and Communication Technologies." *The Communication Review* 7, no. 1 (2004): 3–14.

Lochhead, Judy. "The Sublime, the Ineffable, and Other Dangerous Aesthetics." *Women and Music: A Journal of Gender and Culture* 12, no. 1 (2008): 63–74.

[Longinus]. "On the Sublime." In *Loeb Classical Library: Longinus: On the Sublime,* translated by W. H. Fyfe. Cambridge, MA: Harvard University Press, 1999.

Losh, Elizabeth. "Sensing Exigence: A Rhetoric for Smart Objects." *Computational Culture* 5 (2016): 1–22.

MacIntyre, Alasdair. *After Virtue*. Notre Dame, IN: University of Notre Dame Press, 1981.

Maertens, Rakoen, Frederik Anseel, and Sander van der Linden. "Combatting Climate Change Misinformation: Evidence for Longevity of Inoculation and Consensus Messaging Effects." *Journal of Environmental Psychology* 70, 101455 (2020): 1–11.

Maertens, Rakoen, Jon Roozenbeek, Melisa Basol, and Sander van der Linden. "Long-Term Effectiveness of Inoculation Against Misinformation: Three Longitudinal Experiments." *Journal of Experimental Psychology: Applied* 27, no. 1 (2021): 1–16.

Massumi, Brian. "The Future Birth of the Affective Fact: The Political Ontology of Threat." In *The Affect Theory Reader,* edited by Melissa Gregg and Gregory J. Seigworth, 52–70. Durham, NC: Duke University Press, 2010.

The Mayo Foundation for Medical Education and Research. "Skills from Mayo Clinic." Accessed May 19, 2021, https://www.mayoclinic.org/voice/apps.

McCormack, Jon, and Alan Dorin. "Art, Emergence and the Computational Sublime." In *Second Iteration: Conference on Generative Systems in the Electronic Arts*, 67–81. Melbourne, Australia: CEMA, 2001.

149 Works Cited

McGowan, Mary Kate. "On 'Whites Only' Signs and Racist Hate Speech: Verbal Acts of Racial Discrimination." In *Speech and Harm: Controversies Over Free Speech,* edited by Ishani Maitra and Mary Kate McGowan, 121–47. Oxford: Oxford University Press, 2012.

McGuire, William J. "The Effectiveness of Supportive and Refutational Defenses in Immunizing and Restoring Beliefs Against Persuasion." *Sociometry* 24, no. 2 (1961): 184–97.

———. "Inducing Resistance to Persuasion: Some Contemporary Approaches." In *Advances in Experimental Social Psychology,* edited by Leonard Berkowitz, 191–229. New York: Academic Press, 1964.

Metz, Rachel. "Why Microsoft Accidentally Unleased a Neo-Nazi Sexbot." MIT Technology Review, March 24, 2016. technologyreview.com.

Meyer, Joachim, Chris Miller, Peter Hancock, Ewart J. de Visser, and Michael Dorneich. "Politeness in Machine-Human and Human-Human Interaction." *Proceedings of the Human Factors and Ergonomics Society 2016 Annual Meeting* 60, no. 1 (2016): 279–83.

Miller, Carolyn R. "A Humanistic Rationale for Technical Writing." *College English* 40, no. 6 (1979): 610–17.

———. "Opportunity, Opportunism, and Progress: Kairos in the Rhetoric of Technology." *Argumentation* 8, no. 1 (1994): 81–96.

———. "Technology as a Form of Consciousness: A Study of Contemporary Ethos." *Central States Speech Journal* 29, no. 4 (1978): 228–36.

———. "What Can Automation Tell Us About Agency?" *Rhetoric Society Quarterly* 37, no. 2 (2007): 137–57.

Miner, Adam S., Liliana Laranjo, and A. Baki Kocaballi. "Chatbots in the Fight Against the COVID-19 Pandemic." *npj Digital Medicine* 3, Article 65 (2020): 1–4.

Minsky, Marvin. "Logical Versus Analogical or Symbolic Versus Connectionist or Neat Versus Scruffy." *AI Magazine* 12, no. 2 (1991): 34–51.

Misener, Dan. "Twitter Bot Creates 'remarkably Trump-like' Tweets." CBC News. October 25, 2016. www.cbc.ca/news/science/.

Mitchell, William John Thomas. *What Do Pictures Want? The Lives and Loves of Images.* Chicago: University of Chicago Press, 2005.

Mosco, Vincent. *The Digital Sublime: Myth, Power, and Cyberspace.* Cambridge, MA: MIT Press, 2005.

Motta, Matthew, Timothy Callaghan, and Steven Sylvester. "Knowing Less but Presuming More: Dunning-Kruger Effects and the Endorsement of Anti-Vaccine Policy Attitudes." *Social Science & Medicine* 211 (2018): 274–81.

Muckelbauer, John. "Implicit Paradigms of Rhetorics: Aristotelian, Cultural, and Heliotropic." In *Rhetoric, Through Everyday Things,* edited by Scot Barnett and Casey Boyle, 30–41. Tuscaloosa: University of Alabama Press, 2016.

Mumford, Lewis. *Technics and Civilization.* New York: Harcourt Brace, 1963.

150 Works Cited

Myers, Michael W., and Sara D. Hodges. "Making It Up and Making Do: Simulation, Imagination, and Empathic Accuracy." In *Handbook of Imagination and Mental Simulation,* edited by Keith D. Markman, William M. P. Klein, and Julie A. Suhr, 281–94. New York: Taylor and Francis, 2009.

Nagel, Thomas. "Moral Luck." In *Ethical Theory: An Anthology,* edited by Russ Shaefer-Landau, 322–29. Malden, MA: John Wiley & Sons, 2013.

Nass, Clifford, and Youngme Moon. "Machines and Mindlessness: Social Responses to Computers." *Journal of Social Issues* 56, no. 1 (2000): 81–103.

National Vaccine Information Center. "Biography, Chris Downey MS." 2018. http://www.nvic.org/about/.

Neapolitan, Richard E., and Xia Jiang. *Contemporary Artificial Intelligence.* Boca Raton, FL: CRC Press, 2013.

Neff, Gina, and Peter Nagy. "Talking to Bots: Symbiotic Agency and the Case of Tay." *International Journal of Communication* 10 (2016): 4915–31.

Noble, Safiya Umoja. *Algorithms of Oppression: How Search Engines Reinforce Racism.* New York: New York University Press, 2018.

Nobles, Alicia L., Eric C. Leas, Theodore L. Caputi, Shu-Hong Zhu, Steffanie A. Strathdee, and John W. Ayers. "Responses to Addiction Help-Seeking from Alexa, Siri, Google Assistant, Cortana, and Bixby Intelligent Virtual Assistants." *npj Digital Medicine* 3, Article 11 (2020): 1–3.

Norman, Don. *The Design of Everyday Things.* New York: Basic Books, 2013.

Nye, David E. *American Technological Sublime.* Cambridge, MA: MIT Press, 1996.

Ore, Ersula. "The Lost Cause, Trump Time, and the Necessity of Impatience." *Rhetoric Society Quarterly* 51, no. 3 (2021): 237–39.

Orsagos, Patrick. "No, Amazon's Alexa Doesn't Say 'the Government' Planned the Coronavirus Pandemic." PolitiFact, April 16, 2020, https://www.politifact.com.

Panikkar, Raimundo. "The Destiny of Technological Civilization: An Ancient Buddhist Legend Romavisaya." *Alternatives* 10, no. 2 (1984): 237–53.

Paramount Pictures. Star Trek, the next Generation. Season 7. [United States] Paramount Pictures, 2002. www.imdb.com/title/tt0092455.

Pariser, Eli. *The Filter Bubble: How the New Personalized Web Is Changing What We Read and How We Think.* London: Penguin, 2011.

Parrish, Allison. "Task Complete." Decontextualize, June 6, 2014, accessed July 28, 2017. http://www.decontextualize.com/.

Patterson, Robert E. "Intuitive Cognition and Models of Human-Automation Interaction." *Human Factors* 59, no. 1 (2017): 101–15.

Peirce, Charles Sanders. "What Is a Sign?" In *Theorizing Communication: Reading Across Traditions,* edited by Robert T. Craig and Heidi L. Muller, 177–82. Thousand Oaks, CA: Sage Publications, 2007.

Perdue, Peter C. "Technological Determinism in Agrarian Societies." In *Does Technology*

151 Works Cited

Drive History? edited by Leo Marx and Merritt R. Smith, 169–200. Cambridge, MA: MIT Press, 1994.

Peters, John Durham. *The Marvelous Clouds.* Chicago: University of Chicago Press, 2015.

Pfau, Michael, and Michael Burgoon. "Inoculation in Political Campaign Communication." *Human Communication Research* 15, no. 1 (1988): 91–111.

Potter, Jonathan, Margaret Wetherell, and Andrew Chitty. "Quantification Rhetoric—Cancer on Television." *Discourse & Society* 2, no. 3 (1991): 333–65.

Prior, Markus. "Media and Political Polarization," *Annual Review of Political Science* 16 (2013): 101–27.

Quintilian. *Institutio Oratoria,* Book 2, 1:16 [Online]. Edited by Harold Edgeworth Butler. http://www.perseus.tufts.edu/hopper/.

Ratcliffe, Matthew. "Why Mood Matters." In *Cambridge Companion to Heidegger's Being and Time,* edited by Mark A. Wrathall, 157–76. New York: Cambridge University Press, 2013.

Reeves, Joshua. "Automatic for the People: The Automation of Communicative Labor." *Communication and Critical/Cultural Studies* 13, no. 2 (2016): 150–65.

Rettie, Hannah, and Jo Daniels. "Coping and Tolerance of Uncertainty: Predictors and Mediators of Mental Health During the COVID-19 Pandemic." *American Psychologist* 76, no. 3 (2020): 427–37.

Reyes, G. Mitchell. "The Horizons of Judgement in Mathematical Discourse: Copulas, Economics, and Subprime Mortgages." In *Arguing with Numbers: The Intersections of Rhetoric and Mathematics,* edited by James Wynn and G. Mitchell Reyes, 82–121. University Park: The Pennsylvania University Press, 2021.

———. "The Rhetoric in Mathematics: Newton, Leibniz, the Calculus, and the Rhetorical Force of the Infinitesimal." *Quarterly Journal of Speech* 90, no. 2 (2004): 163–88.

Reyman, Jessica. "The Rhetorical Agency of Algorithms." In *Theorizing Digital Rhetoric,* edited by Aaron Hess and Amber Davisson, 112–25. London: Routledge, 2018.

Reyman, Jessica, and Erika M. Sparby. "Introduction: Toward an Ethic of Responsibility in Digital Aggression." In *Digital Ethics: Rhetoric and Responsibility in Online Aggression,* edited by Jessica Reyman and Erika M. Sparby, 1–14. New York: Routledge, 2019.

Rice, Jenny. "The Rhetorical Aesthetics of More: On Archival Magnitude." *Philosophy & Rhetoric* 50, no. 1 (2017): 26–49.

Richards, Riley J., Patric R. Spence, and Chad Edwards. "Human-Machine Communication Scholarship Trends: An Examination of Research From 2011 to 2021 in Communication Journals." *Human–Machine Communication* 4, no. 1 (2022): 45–62.

Rickert, Thomas J. *Ambient Rhetoric: The Attunements of Rhetorical Being.* Pittsburgh, PA: University of Pittsburgh Press, 2013.

———. "Preliminary Steps Toward a General Rhetoric: Existence, Thrivation, Transformation." In *Handbook on Comparative Rhetoric,* edited by Keith Lloyd, 414–21. New York: Routledge, 2020.

Robertson, Adi. "Your Favorite Twitter Bot Might Die Next Week." *The Verge*, February 2, 2023. www.theverge.com/2023/2/2/23582982/.

Robinson, Abby. "Online Tool Creates Catch-Up Immunization Schedules for Missed Childhood Vaccinations." *Horizons*, April 1, 2022. https://rh.gatech.edu.

Rojas, Raúl, and Ulf Hashagen. *The First Computers: History and Architectures.* Cambridge, MA: MIT Press, 2000.

Roland, Alex, and Philip Shiman. *Strategic Computing: DARPA and the Quest for Machine Intelligence, 1983–1993.* Cambridge, MA: MIT Press, 2002.

Roose, Kevin. "A Conversation with Bing's Chatbot Left Me Deeply Unsettled." *New York Times*, February 16, 2023.

Roundtree, Aimee Kendall. *Computer Simulation, Rhetoric, and the Scientific Imagination: How Virtual Evidence Shapes Science in the Making and in the News.* Lanham, MD: Lexington Books, 2013.

Rudschies, Catharina, Ingrid Schneider, and Judith Simon. "Value Pluralism in the AI Ethics Debate–Different Actors, Different Priorities." *The International Review of Information Ethics* 29 (2020): 1–15.

"schedule-service.js" [JavaScript File]. Vaccine Scheduler, accessed March 2018, https://web.archive.org/web/20180322130655/https://vacscheduler.org/.

Schlesinger, Ari, Kenton P. O'Hara, and Alex S. Taylor. "Let's Talk About Race: Identity, Chatbots, and AI." In *Proceedings of the 2018 CHI Conference on Human Factors in Computing Systems*, 1–14. New York: ACM, 2018.

Schwartz, Eric Hal. "EXCLUSIVE: Amazon Alexa Has Removed Coronavirus Skills and Won't Approve New Ones." VoiceBot, March 17, 2020. https://voicebot.ai/2020/03/17/.

Seeger, Anna-Maria, and Armin Heinzl. "Human Versus Machine: Contingency Factors of Anthropomorphism as a Trust-Inducing Design Strategy for Conversational Agents." In *Lecture Notes in Information Systems and Organization* 25, edited by Fred D. Davis, René Riedl, Jan vom Brocke, Pierre-Majorique Léger, and Adriane B. Randolph, 129–39. Cham, Switzerland: Springer International, 2018.

Sezgin, Emre, Yungui Huang, Ujjwal Ramtekkar, and Simon Lin. "Readiness for Voice Assistants to Support Healthcare Delivery During a Health Crisis and Pandemic." *npj Digital Medicine* 3, Article 122 (2020): 1–4.

Shah, Saquib. "Microsoft's 'Zo' Chatbot Picked up Some Offensive Habits." Engadget, April 4, 201. www.engadget.com.

Shead, Sam. "Here's Why Microsoft's Teen Chatbot Turned into a Genocidal Racist, According to an AI Expert." *Business Insider*, March 24, 2016. www.businessinsider.com.

Silva, Cristina. "Who Won the Republican Debate Saturday? Donald Trump Is a Winner because Marco Rubio Had a Bad Night." *International Business Times*, February 6, 2016. www.ibtimes.com.

153   Works Cited

Simis, Molly J., Haley Madden, Michael A. Cacciatore, and Sara K. Yeo. "The Lure of Rationality: Why Does the Deficit Model Persist in Science Communication?" *Public Understanding of Science* 25, no. 4 (2016): 400–414.

Smalley, Hannah K., Pinar Keskinocak, Faramroze G. Engineer, and Larry K. Pickering. "Universal Tool for Vaccine Scheduling: Applications for Children and Adults." *Interfaces* 41, no. 5 (2011): 436–54.

Socher, Richard, Alex Perelygin, Jean Y. Wu, Jason Chuang, Christopher D. Manning, Andrew Y. Ng, and Christopher Potts. "Recursive Deep Models for Semantic Compositionality Over a Sentiment Treebank." In *Proceedings of the 2013 Conference on Empirical Methods in Natural Language Processing,* edited by David Yarowsky, Timothy Baldwin, Anna Korhonen, Karen Livescu, and Steven Bethard, 1631–42. Stroudsburg, PA: Association for Computation Linguistics, 2013.

Soper, Taylor. "Amazon Alexa Leader: COVID-19 Has Sparked a Huge Increase in the Use of Voice in the Home." GeekWire, June 25, 2020, https://www.geekwire.com/2020.

Spice, Byron. "Most Presidential Candidates Speak at Grade 6–8." Carnegie Mellon University, March 16, 2016. www.cmu.edu/news/stories/archives/2016/march/speechifying.html.

Spinuzzi, Clay. "'Light Green Doesn't Mean Hydrology!': Toward a Visual–Rhetorical Framework for Interface Design." *Computers and Composition* 18, no. 1 (2001): 39–53.

Staff and Agencies. "Microsoft 'Deeply Sorry' for Racist and Sexist Tweets by AI Chatbot." *The Guardian*, March 26, 2016. www.theguardian.com.

Strong, John S. "Aśoka and the Buddha Relics." In *Relics of the Buddha*, 124–49. Princeton, NJ: Princeton University Press, 2004.

Sullivan, Dale. "The Epideictic Rhetoric of Science." *Journal of Business and Technical Communication* 5, no. 3 (1991): 229–45.

Swaim, Barton. "How Donald Trump's Language Works for Him." *Washington Post*, September 15, 2015, https://www.washingtonpost.com/news/the-fix/wp/2015/09/15/.

Szolovits, Peter. "Knowledge-Based Systems: A Survey." In *On Knowledge Base Management Systems: Integrating Artificial Intelligence and Database Technologies*, edited by Michael L. Brodie and John Mylopoulos, 339–52. New York: Springer-Verlag, 1986.

Tal, Aner, and Brian Wansink. "Blinded with Science: Trivial Graphs and Formulas Increase Ad Persuasiveness and Belief in Product Efficacy." *Public Understanding of Science* 25, no. 1 (2016): 117–25.

Turkle, Sherry. *Alone Together: Why We Expect More from Technology and Less from Each Other.* New York: Basic Books, 2012.

Twitter. Twitter API. Accessed May 20, 2023, https://developer.twitter.com/en/products/twitter-api.

154 Works Cited

U.S. Census Bureau. "2013 ACS 1-year Public Use Microdata Samples," accessed July 28, 2017. https://factfinder.census.gov/faces/nav/jsf/pages/searchresults.xhtml?refresh=t.

U.S. Food and Drug Administration. "Engerix-B, Package Insert," retrieved May 4, 2018. https://www.fda.gov/media/119403/download.

Vaccine Ingredients Calculator. "About the Vaccine Ingredients Calculator." April 20, 2018, http://vaxcalc.org.

———. "Discover the Ingredients in the Vaccines that Your Doctor Recommends." retrieved April 20, 2018, http://vaxcalc.org.

———. "STEP 1 of 2: Tell Us About Who is Being Vaccinated." retrieved April 20, 2018, https://vaxcalc.org/calc-step-1.

———. "STEP 2: Choose Vaccines for [Name]." retrieved April 20, 2018, https://vaxcalc.org/calc-step-2.

van der Linden, Sander, Anthony Leiserowitz, Seth Rosenthal, and Edward Maibach. "Inoculating the Public Against Misinformation about Climate Change." *Global Challenges* 1 (2017): 1–7.

van der Linden, Sander, and Jon Roozenbeek. "Psychological Inoculation Against Fake News." In *The Psychology of Fake News: Accepting, Sharing, and Correcting Misinformation,* edited by Rainer Greifeneder, Mariela Jaffe, Eryn Newman, and Norbert Schwarz, 147–69. London: Routledge, 2021.

van der Linden, Sander, Jon Roozenbeek, and Josh Compton. "Inoculating Against Fake News About COVID-19." *Frontiers in Psychology* 11, 566790 (2020): 1–7.

VaxCalc-Labs. "vaccine-ingredients-data," May 11, 2016, GitHub, retrieved May 3, 2018, https://github.com/VaxCalc-Labs.

Vee, Annette. *Coding Literacy: How Computer Programming Is Changing Writing.* Cambridge, MA: MIT Press, 2017.

———. "Full Stack Rhetoric: A Response to *Rhetorical Machines*." In *Rhetorical Machines: Writing, Code, and Computational Ethics,* edited by John Jones and Livinia Hirsu, 237–44. Tuscaloosa: University of Alabama Press, 2019.

Vee, Annette, and James J. Brown Jr. "Rhetoric Special Issue Editorial Introduction." *Computational Culture* 5 (2016): 1–20.

Veruggio, Gianmarco, and Fiorella Operto. "Roboethics: Social and Ethical Implications of Robotics." In *Springer Handbook of Robotics,* edited by Bruno Sciliano and Oussama Khatib, 2135–60. New York: Springer, 2008.

Walker, Jeffrey. *Rhetoric and Poetics in Antiquity.* New York: Oxford University Press, 2000.

Walsh, Lynda. *Scientists as Prophets: A Rhetorical Genealogy.* New York: Oxford University Press, 2013.

Walton, Douglas. *Ad Hominem Arguments.* Tuscaloosa: University of Alabama Press, 1998.

155   Works Cited

Wardrip-Fruin, Noah. *Expressive Processing: Digital Fictions, Computer Games, and Software Studies.* Cambridge, MA: MIT Press, 2009.

Weizenbaum, Joseph. *Computer Power and Human Reason: From Judgement to Calculation.* New York: W. H. Freeman, 1976.

Wikipedia. "About," accessed March 21, 2021. https://en.wikipedia.org/.

Williams, Bernard A. O., and Thomas Nagel. "Moral Luck." *Proceedings of the Aristotelian Society, Supplementary Volumes* 50 (1976): 115–35.

Winston, Brian. "Mechanising Calculation." In *Media, Technology, and Society: A History from the Telegraph to the Internet,* 147–65. London: Routledge, 2003.

Wise, J. Macgregor. "Towards a Minor Assemblage: An Introduction to the Clickable World." In *Theorizing Digital Rhetoric,* edited by Aaron Hess and Amber Davisson, 68–82. New York: Routledge, 2018.

Wood, Michelle L. M. "Rethinking the Inoculation Analogy: Effects on Subjects with Differing Preexisting Attitudes." *Human Communication Research* 33, no. 3 (2007): 357–78.

Woods, Heather Suzanne. "Asking More of Siri and Alexa: Feminine Persona in Service of Surveillance Capitalism." *Critical Studies in Media Communication* 35, no. 4 (2018): 334–49.

World Health Organization. "Coronavirus Disease 2019 (COVID-19) Situation Report—86." April 15, 2020. https://www.who.int/docs/default-source/coronaviruse/situation-reports/.

Wynn, James. *Citizen Science in the Digital Age: Rhetoric, Science, and Public Engagement.* Tuscaloosa: University of Alabama Press, 2017.

Yasuoka, Koichi, and Motoko Yasuoka. "On the Prehistory of QWERTY." *ZINBUN* 42 (2011): 161–74.

Yoston Lawrence, Heidi. *Vaccine Rhetorics.* Columbus: The Ohio State University Press, 2020.

Zagacki, Kenneth S., and Victoria J. Gallagher. "Rhetoric and Materiality in the Museum Park at the North Carolina Museum of Art." *Quarterly Journal of Speech* 95, no. 2 (2009): 171–91.

Zarocostas, John. "How to Fight an Infodemic." *The Lancet* 395, no. 10225 (2020): 676.

Zhang, Jia. "Introducing censusAmericans, a Twitter Bot for America." FiveThirtyEight, accessed July 28, 2017. https://fivethirtyeight.com.

Ziewitz, Malte. "Governing Algorithms: Myth, Mess, and Methods." *Science, Technology, & Human Values* 41, no. 1 (2016): 3–16.

INDEX

Italicized page numbers indicate illustrations.

Abbate, Janet, 74
Adams, Douglas, 24
affective compulsion, 64, 65–74, 86–87; and human reactions to machines, 72–73
Akerkar, Rajendra A., 28
Alexa (Amazon), 105–7; contrasted with Oracle of Delphia, 119; health apps during COVID-19 pandemic, 115–16; rhetorical energies of, 119–20, 123
algorithms, 48–49, 94
Amazon's Alexa. *See* Alexa (Amazon)
Ambient Rhetoric (Rickert), 15, 59
Ames, Morgan, 48
Amoore, Louise, 92
analytic reasoning, 42
Anderson, Wayne, 82
angst, 57–59
anthropomechanation, 116–17
anthropomorphism, 33
Antonelli, Kay McNulty Mauchly, 74
archival magnitude, 46–47, 82
Aristotle, 10, 46, 81
artificial intelligence (AI): symbolic vs. connectionist, 28–29; writing by, 64–65
attunements, 15–17, 20, 54, 58–59, 85
AutoSpeech-Easy, 7–8

Baldwin, Alec, 68, 81

Banas, John A., 122
Banks, Jaime, 117
Barad, Karen, 12
Barnett, Scot, 4
Bartik, Jean Jennings, 74
Bilas, Frances (Spence), 74
bird populations, 60–61
Bogost, Ian, 18
Bollinger, Lee C., 106
Bowden, Bertram Vivian, 75–76
Boyle, Casey, 4, 11, 20
Bradshaw, Jonathan, 47
Brock, Kevin, 19, 60
Brown, James J., 11, 17, 18–19, 22, 99
Brunner, Elizabeth, 95
Burroughs, William S., 70
Burtynsky, Edward, 55
Bush, Vannevar, 75

Čapek, Karel, 88
carbon footprint software, 19–20, *21*
Carey, James W., 48
Carey, Tamika L., 107
Catch-Up Vaccine Scheduler, 29–33, *31, 34;* comparison with Vaccine Calculator, 35. *See also* Vaccine Calculator
Ceccarelli, Leah, 7, 23
@censusAmericans, 45, 48, 49–61, 110
Ceraso, Steph, 11
Chaput, Catherine, 6, 17, 79

158 Index

chatbots, 12–13; medical applications, 113–114; and moral luck, 91; and moral programming, 95–96
Christ of the Abyss (Galletti), 45
citizen science, 44
Cloud Ethics (Amoore), 92
coherentization, 47
Coleman, E. Gabriella, 86
Colombini, Crystal Broch, 6, 79
communication, human-machine. *See* human-machine communication
"compulsion" contrasted with "impulse," 66. *See also* affective compulsion
Computational Culture (journal), 17
computing machines: as active agents, 1–2; agency of, 11–12; deep end, realm of, 13–18, 20, 67, 72–74, 86–87, 110–113; and energies, positive and negative, 92–93; ethics of responsibility, 98–102; first- and second-order agency, 93–95; front end contrasted with back end, 13–15, 110; information processing and storage, 13; and moral agency, 107–9; moral praise and blame, 88–89, 90–93; performative energy, 13–18; procedural rhetoric, 18–23, *21;* rhetorical energies of, 5–13; and science communication, 24–27, 39; user interface, 13
connectionist artificial intelligence, 28–29
conspiracy theories, 40, 121
constraints, 23, 53
COVID-19 pandemic: and health apps, 115–16; "infodemic," 112–16
Crick, Nathan, 66
Critique of the Power of Judgement (Kant), 47

@DeepDrumpf, 66, *82, 83, 85,* 111; analysis of, 79–86; model, structural, 77–78
de Graaf, Maartje, 117
Deleuze, Giles, 55
Dewey, John, 66
digital computing, history of, 74–75

Digital Ethics (Reyman & Sparby), 98
distributed morality, 100–102
Dorin, Alan, 49–50, 53, 54, 56
"double rainbow" video, 62–63
Dunning, David, 41
Dunning-Kruger effect, 40–41
dynamical sublime, 53–54

Edwards, Autumn P., 5
Edwards, Chad, 118
ELIZA effect (ELIZA chatbot), 32, 73
emergence, concept of, 50
emotion contrasted with logic, 15–17
ethics: ethic of responsibility, 98–102; rules-based approaches, 103, 104
expert advice and science communication, 42–44
expert systems, 27–28

feminine personae of voice-based assistants, 106
first-order agency, 93
Fisher, Walter, 70
Floridi, Luciano, 100–101
Fortunati, Leopoldina, 5

Gallagher, Victoria J., 68
Galletti, Guido, 45
Geometry Theorem Prover, 76
Gillespie, Tarleton, 98
GitHub, 51
Gonzatti, Dario, 45
GPT-3, 64–65
"grooves" of culture, 68–69; and neural networks, 74–79
Gross, Daniel, 16
Gunkel, David J., 14, 91, 94, 97
Guzman, Andrea L., 112

"habit" and computational performance, 67
hate speech, 89
"hateware," 99–100

159 Index

Hawhee, Debra, 10, 16, 57, 68–69
Hawk, Byron, 17
Hayes, Bradley, 79–80
Heidegger, Martin, 15–17
Hennis, Gregory, 99
Henriques, Julian, 68
The Hitchhiker's Guide to the Galaxy (Adams), 24
Hodges, Sara D., 58
Holberton, Betty Snyder, 74
Holmes, Steve, 67
Homer, 57–58
"A Hoot in the Dark" (Kennedy), 2, 19
Horner, David S., 96
human-machine communication, 5–6, 112–13, 132n28; persuasive roles for machines, 114–115; and rhetorical energies, 117–21. *See also* chatbots
Human-Machine Communication (journal), 5
human-nature interface, 68

Illiad (Homer), 57
images, physical responses to, 70
"impulse" contrasted with "compulsion," 66
infinity: "at work," 46, 53, 56, 57, 58, 59–60, 110; concept of, 53–54, 56
Ingraham, Chris, 6
inoculation theory, 121–24
interface archaeology, 26–27

Jennings, Jean (Bartik), 74
Jones, Hillary A., 41
joy, experience of, 62–63

Kane, Carolyn, 55, 57
Kang, Minsoo, 56
Kant, Immanuel, 47; Kantian frameworks, 53; Kant's sublime, 54–55
Kazemi, Darius, 57
Kennedy, George, 2–3, 6–7, 10, 19
Kennedy, Krista, 9–10, 12

King, Preston, 106
knowledge-based systems, 27–34
Kocaballi, A. Baki, 115
Kruger, Justin, 41

language, kinetic energy, and metaphor, 10–11
Laranjo, Liliana, 115
Larson, Stephanie, 47
Lawrence, Heidi Yoston, 40
Lewis, Seth C., 112
Lichterman, Ruth (Teitelbaum), 74
limits of avoidance, 95–98
logic contrasted with emotion, 16–17
logistical media, 71
Lokapannati, 1
Longinus, 57–58

machine-learning, probability contrasted with deduction, 76–77
machinic intervention, paradox of, 102–5
MacIntyre, Alasdair, 70
magical thinking, 69–70
magnitude: archival magnitude, 46–47, 82; processual magnitude, 46, 59–61, 111
manufactured processing as tactic, 24–27
Massumi, Brian, 40
mathematical sublime, 53–54
mathematics and rhetoric, 76–79
mattering contrasted with matter, 12
Mayo Clinic, 115–16
McCormack, Jon, 49–50, 53, 54, 56
McNulty, Kay (Mauchly Antonelli), 74
Meltzer, Marlyn Wescoff, 74
meta-ignorance, 41
metaphor and kinetic energy, 10–11
#MeToo hashtag, 47
Microsoft's Taybot (chatbot), 89, 97–98
Miller, Carolyn R., 7–9, 81
Miner, Adam S., 115
misinformation, 113–16, 121–24
Mitchell, William J. T., 69–70

Moon, Youngme, 32–33
moral luck, 90–93; and Amazon's Alexa, 105–7; and limits of avoidance, 95–98
Mosco, Vincent, 48
Muckelbaurer, John, 4
Myers, Michael W., 58

Nass, Clifford, 32–33
natural phenomena, reactions to, 62–65, 72, 87. *See also* affective compulsion
neural networks, 66, 74–79
Nietzsche, Friedrich, 66
Norman, Don, 71
Nye, David, 48

Oliver, John, 80
On the Sublime (Hawhee), 57
Operto, Fiorella, 103
Oracle of Delphi, 113, 117, 118–19

parody, 80. *See also* @DeepDrumpf
Parrish, Allison, 51
Peirce, Charles S., 69
Persuasive Games (Bogost), 18
Peters, John Durham, 70–71
poiesis, 50, 53, 56–57
precautionary principle, 102–5
procedural enthymemes, 19
procedural habits, 67
procedural rhetorics, 3–4, 18–23, *21*
processual magnitude, 46, 59–61, 111
processual signaling, 64, 111; critique of, 86–87
prophetic ethos, 26
Pythia, 118

Quinn, Zoe, 97
Quintilian, 107
Quirk, John J., 48

racism, tolerance for, 106–7
Rains, Stephen A., 122
Rambot, 9

Ramsey, Derek, 9
Ratcliffe, Matthew, 58
Recoding Gender (Abbate), 74
reiteration, rhetoric of, 81–82
resonance, 17, 72, 73
responsibility, ethic of distributed, 98–102
Reyes, Mitchell, 78
Reyman, Jessica, 98, 100, 108
rheme (unit of measure), 3
rhetoric: definitions of, 107; expansion of, 4; and mathematics, 76–79; procedural rhetoric, 18–23, *21*
Rhetoric (Aristotle), 10
Rhetoric, Through Everyday Things (Barnett & Boyle), 4
Rhetorica Ad Herennium, 53
rhetorical energies, 2–3; of computing machines, 5–13; and misinformation, 121–24; traditional vs. computational performances, 7–9, *8*
Rhetorical Machines: Writing, Code, and Computational Ethics (Jones & Hirsu), 22
Rhetoric in Tooth and Claw (Hawhee), 10
rhythm and vibration, 68–69
Rice, Jenny, 46, 82
Rickert, Thomas, 14–15, 17, 59
robot speech, perceptions of, 116–17
Rossum's Universal Robots (Čapek), 88
Roundtree, Aimee K., 43
Rudschies, Catharina, 108

Sajja, Priti Srinivas, 28
Schneider, Ingrid, 108
science: citizen science, 44; expert advice and science communication, 42–44; "signaling" and science communication, 24–27, 39
science denial, 46–47
Scientists as Prophets (Walsh), 26
second-order agency, 93–94
sensation and language, 10, 16–17, 125n7
Shepherd, Dawn, 19

161 Index

Simon, Judith, 108
Snyder, Betty (Holberton), 74
social media platforms, 41–42; custodian metaphor, 99
spaces of attention, 68
Sparby, Erika M., 98, 100, 108
species loss, 60–61
Spence, Frances Bilas, 74
Spinuzzi, Clay, 26
Stein, Jill, 84, 85
"Stimmung" (Heidegger), 15–17
storytelling, importance of, 70–71
Strategic Computing Initiative, 76
Sublime Dreams of Living Machines (Kang), 56
sublimity, 45–61
Sullivan, Dale, 84
symbolic artificial intelligence, 28–29
symbolic associations, 69–70
symbolic interaction, 5–6
System 2 reasoning, 42

Tal, Aner, 25–26
Taybot (chatbot), 89, 97–98, 135n10
Taylor, Tom, 121
Teitelbaum, Ruth Lichterman, 74
Tiainen, Milla, 68
tolerance and free speech, 106–7
transduction, metaphor of, 11
Trump, Donald, 79–80; speaking style, 84. *See also* @DeepDrumpf
Twitter, bot culture, 2, 7, 22, 49, 51–52, 131n57. *see also* @censusAmericans; @DeepDrumpf

Vaccine Calculator, 29, 34–44, *36, 37,* 86, 110, 120
Väliaho, Pasi, 68
Vasquez, Paul "Bear," 62–63
Vee, Annette, 14, 17
Veruggio, Gianmarco, 103
vibration and rhythm, 68–69
video games, 18

Walker, Jeffrey, 20
Walsh, Lynda, 26
Walton, Douglas, 81
Wansink, Brian, 25–26
Wardrip-Fruin, Noah, 32
Watson Assistant for Citizens (IBM), 114
Weizenbaum, Joseph, 73
Wescoff, Marlyn (Meltzer), 74
Wikipedia articles, 9–10, 78, 119, 124
Woods, Heather Suzanne, 106
writing process, 9–10
wrongdoing: avoidance of deliberate, 102; communicative by machinic agents, 103; by machines, 89, 91, 94, 95–97, 101–2
Wynn, James, 44

X-ray sublime, 55, 56, 59

Yasuoka, Koichi, 71
Yasuoka, Motoko, 71

Zagacki, Kenneth S., 68
Zhang, Jia, 49, 51–53, 57, 60
Zo (chatbot), 89